The Last Years of WALKER EVANS

Martha's Vineyard,
Massachusetts,
October, 1974

The Last Years of **WALKER EVANS**

a first-hand account by **Jerry L. Thompson**

with 35 illustrations, 8 in color

Thames and Hudson

All photographs not otherwise credited are by the author.

First published in the United States of America in 1997 by Thames and Hudson Inc.,
500 Fifth Avenue, New York, New York 10110

Library of Congress Catalog Card Number 97-60243
ISBN 0-500-54210-4

Printed and bound in Hong Kong

for LESLIE KATZ

A *A violent order is disorder; and*
B *A great disorder is an order. These*
    Two things are one.
    (Pages of illustrations.)

Wallace Stevens

SINCE HIS DEATH in 1975, much has been written about Walker Evans, but little attention has been directed to his final years. So far, students of this American artist have slighted, if not ignored, the events and work of his late life.

In reading posthumous accounts of Evans, I have often been struck – forcefully – that some essentials are missing: a sense of the presence of the man himself, with his complexity, contradictions, and many qualities, and also an accurate estimate of the subtlety and reach of his artistic work – particularly the work of the last three years, the part of his life I knew first-hand. For at least fifteen years I have been writing letters to students of Evans (as well as to some editors) in attempts to correct what I knew to be omissions or understood as misconceptions. As a recent letter grew to the length of a small essay, I decided simply to write out the story of the last years of his life myself, as I knew it.

Many other people were connected to Evans during the years I knew him, a number quite closely. I have not tried to compare my memories with theirs, or to ask about events I did not witness. Rather than attempt to sift and blend disparate memories into a smooth rounded account, I have chosen to rely on first-hand knowledge. I have consulted only the few notes I made at the time, letters I had received from Evans, a number of photographs, and my memory.

I have confined myself to events I took part in or heard about from Evans, opinions I remember forming at the time, and some broader conclusions I have been unavoidably drawn to over the years.

As self-reliant as it is, this essay (and its author) owe two large debts. The first is to John Hill, the friend chosen by Evans to be the executor of his estate, who regularly involved me in the plans for publishing and preserving Evans's work initiated by the estate during its twenty years of independent existence. Conversations with John Hill helped to keep my interest in Evans fresh, and – more importantly – his unsurpassed knowledge of the man and his work has greatly enlarged my own understanding of Evans as an artist.

The other large debt is to Maria Morris Hambourg and Jeff Rosenheim of the Metropolitan Museum of Art. When they acquired the estate in 1994 they kindly invited me to look at the Polaroid SX-70 pictures made by Evans during the time I knew him. During several sessions in the Museum's print study room I had the great pleasure of re-seeing hundreds of pictures I first saw more than twenty years ago, as they were being made, most of which have not been available for viewing since.

One person's view cannot supply the whole story, perhaps not even the last word on the subject. But I saw a lot, and I was paying close attention. This account at least avoids the error of examining selected biographical details of Evans's late years while failing to take sufficient notice of the work he was doing at the time – a mistake, with the Evans I knew, comparable to failing to notice whether he was breathing. His main interest, his chief commitment, when I knew him, was to be an artist, as anyone would know who ever heard him say the word, stretching the first syllable to savor the resonance of the vowel, softening the *r* and gently nudging *ar* toward *ah*, his voice projecting an aura so pronounced as to be almost visible in the air.

IN THE FALL of 1973, when I began to teach at Yale, I was living in Walker Evans's Connecticut house in Old Lyme. As the end of summer had approached, Evans was preparing to leave on a trip to England, and I was staying on as long as possible in a rented room in Brooklyn, New York, where I was photographing, spending on 8 x 10 film what savings I had left from graduate school, and postponing making plans for housing in New Haven in the fall. My salary wouldn't start until after I began teaching.

Though I had known Evans for less than two years, we had been through a lot, and our friendship, at this time, was easygoing. He suggested that I could stay in his house rent-free – he would be away for much of September, anyway – and then I could find a place of my own later on, maybe a place in New Haven where he might visit overnight from time to time. He was officially retired by then from the university faculty – Yale had a mandatory retirement policy at that time – but drove the forty miles from Old Lyme into New Haven frequently.

My teaching job, that first year, was cobbled together from several small budget items, one of them a reduced version of the position left vacant by Evans's retirement. My schedule was consequently a little uneven, and on one or two days I had morning classes, afternoon appointments, and a late class that met after dinner. On those days I left Old Lyme early and wound up making the hour-long drive back late at night.

After Evans returned from England in late September, we shared his house and had frequent talks. Once I mentioned to him that on my late-night drives home I found I was too tired to think out anything at all that was complicated. I would dwell on some unresolved question, mulling it over and over but unable to come to any conclusion. I was then 28 and was discovering for the first time that I could think better at the beginning than at the end of a long day.

In response, Evans asked me to imagine that I felt just that tired and muddled first thing in the morning on the best days of my life. That, he said, was what it felt like to be his age. He was then 69.

I MET WALKER EVANS in the fall of 1971 in New Haven, where I had gone for a graduate course in photography at the Yale School of Art. Evans was the senior figure there, and I had tried to meet him before actually enrolling; but he had never been available on a day when I was visiting. So in September 1971, after resigning a full-time job teaching sixth-graders in New York City and selling the photographer's studio I lived in, I finally came to meet the man I hoped would play a large role in my advanced education.

A few days after I arrived I learned that admission to Evans's class was not automatic, even for graduate students; he interviewed all prospective students before admitting them into his course. This news was not welcome; I had made large adjustments to be here to study with him, and I had already turned down another offer of admission. I reviewed my entire modest achievement in photography to prepare for this interview, rearranging the order of my prints in an attempt to make the strongest case for admission to his class. I was worried.

At the appointed day and hour I stood in a small outer office, next to the departmental secretary's desk, while Evans finished another interview out of my sight, in an inner conference room. I got a signal from the secretary to go in, but a second-year student jumped ahead of me, saying he wanted to say hello and ask "Walker how his summer was."

Already ridiculously overwrought, I was even further keyed up by this unexpected delay and the casualness with which it had been administered. My case of nerves was fueled by several years of wanting to do something serious in photography – something connected to some real world, not just my anonymous amateur studio – and several months of wanting to do it here, at Yale, with Evans. When my time finally came I burst into the conference room where I saw a small, nervous-looking man dressed in a tweed jacket, sweater, and tie. He had a thermos and a cup of tea before him on the table, and he seemed vaguely afraid of something.

At his invitation I sat down, focussing all my attention on this long-awaited meeting. I must have displayed more excitement at this encounter than he (or anyone else) thought reasonable. I was ready to explode with words and sequenced prints as soon as he asked me about my proposed work for his class, but he didn't ask. Instead he astonished me by asking where I was in the university.

I was a graduate student, I said, amazed that he didn't know, since only four were admitted in photography each year.

Oh? He asked with faint interest, In what?

Evans in New Haven, late 1971 or early 1972, photographed by John T. Hill

In what? In photography, I answered with growing anxiety.

I didn't know they took graduate students in photography, he said conversationally, without any emphasis or surprise.

This remark routed all my preparations. When he asked whether the prints I had were for him to look at, I dumbly began to take the top off the 6-inch-thick box without giving my prepared pitch. The prints were in glassine envelopes, and I began to remove the first from its translucent sheath.

Oh man, I've seen enough, he said before the print was fully out of its envelope. Anyone who can print like that has a place in my class.

My interview was over.

I knew that Evans was an accomplished photographer – I had seen his pictures, and people I respected confirmed my admiration. My prior experience in graduate school led me

Evans talking to Yale students, Norfolk, CT, July, 1972

to expect that he would feel obliged to make a good photographer out of me, too.

My previous graduate professors, all scholars, had had methods for making us students into scholars. They devised exercises and learning experiences for us. They taught, and they told us what to read. Evans was different, and in class he was as elusive, even evasive, as he had been at my interview. Other faculty members taught things, many things new and of interest to me, but Evans's teaching was mostly conversation, and the conversation frequently led rather far away from photography. Many of the students in his class were Yale undergraduates, some from exotic backgrounds (one lived in a castle in Scotland), and many had traveled. Some had read. Evans tended to draw them out, encouraging them to talk about what they knew – which they did, readily.

I learned that, partly because of his big retrospective show at the Museum of Modern Art in New York earlier that year (1971), Evans's course was what was then known at Yale as a Celebrity Course. There were other such courses, and aggressive undergraduates tried to take as many of them as possible, liberally first-naming the instructors. Evans used his celebrity as a kind of armor, sitting passively inside his reputation while the Yalies chattered away. Other advanced students attended only irregularly, showing up from time to time with a small stack of prints to be admired by the undergraduates and (a little too readily, it seemed to me) by the professor. I sat in a corner and occasionally glowered.

After a few of the weekly meetings I noticed that Evans was never in a hurry to leave at the end of class. He would sit with two or three of the students, continuing to talk after the others left, sometimes, apparently, with great interest. I began to hang around, too, and we talked a little. If he wouldn't teach me anything, at least I could observe him closely. I watched everything he did and said, and I think he noticed. Later on he flattered me by saying that he had been struck by my "intensity."

Evans was scheduled to provide a show that winter for the Yale University Art Gallery, and one of my graduate classmates, Melinda Blauvelt, was to be his assistant. She was to help with the selection and organization of the pictures, but he also needed other kinds of help – lugging boxes, mounting prints, and so on. My classmate suggested, generously, that I too might help. On the basis of this recommendation and our few conversations, Evans asked me if I would do a couple of things for him. I said yes, of course, and accepted his first assignment: to transport a heavy book press from his house to the school print-mounting area.

I can still see in my mind's eye the front porch of the Victorian ark I imagined he must live in. To my surprise the house he led me to was a low, angular structure built in the 1960s with the help of a Yale architect he had known. Though it incorporated such traditional American features as a row of half-pilot lights along one side of the ridgepole – an arrangement sometimes used in factory buildings of the nineteenth century – its spirit was modern. Evans toyed with the idea of calling it *Clerestory* in honor of its high windows.

The furniture I saw was mostly not modern. A corduroy-covered Victorian couch, a plain American hardwood dining table, some ladderback chairs, and a *papier-maché* tea table shared the rooms with eye-catching objects – handsome old instrument cases used as low tables in front of a loveseat, electrified kerosene lamps, a phrenological head and a ceramic hand on end tables. A rack of dark wall-mounted bookcases dominated the living room. Almost all the books were hardcover except for an impressive row of paperback publications of the *Nouvelle Revue Française*, which filled the upper left shelf. There were no photographs or photographic paraphernalia in the living or dining rooms.

The press I was to transport to New Haven was in a large workroom separated from the rest of the house by a door. This studio was lighted from above by the half-pilots, and also by a row of large picture-type windows running the length of the room along the outside wall. The press was on a counter set against this row of windows, and to get to it, I had to thread my way carefully through stacks of Evans's artistic detritus. Prints mounted and unmounted, in boxes and loose stacks, lay on most of the surfaces. Negatives were mainly stored in envelopes in a number of metal boxes, but a few were out in the open. Some of the negative envelopes were marked with the sort of squiggle Evans would make when trying to get a felt-tip pen to started writing.

Other negatives were stored in expanding cardboard files or stashed in briefcases, sometimes without protective envelopes. There was a manuscript box, handmade by a student, containing twenty or thirty varying prints from one negative – test prints for a portfolio just completed. One wooden cabinet, resembling a nightstand, held a great stack of prints of African sculpture. As yet unpacked moving cartons from Evans's last New York address were stored under another counter. Recent collectings – signs and paper ephemera – were beginning to form a thin layer piled on top of everything else. A couple of suitcases were full of mail, some of it unopened.

Exploration of this cave of wonders would come later. That night I carried out the heavy press, along with an indelible impression of what I had glimpsed, and drove back toward New Haven, readjusting my appraisal of the man I was getting to know.

EVANS'S YALE SHOW was to have been called "Walker Evans: An Anthology of Taste," and was to have presented his selection of contemporary photographs made by others. A few selections had been made, some from among pictures students showed him in his seminar, but he apparently had no clear plan in mind. Some deadline must have passed, and the show became "Walker Evans: Forty Years," the second retrospective of his work in 1971. My contribution was to help bring boxes of prints in from Old Lyme, mount some new prints, and do a few other gofer chores requiring some but not much skill or experience.

I began to see more of Evans outside of class and discovered that he often had no one to dine with. Isabelle, his wife, was at the time living in their New York apartment and visited him some weekends. I also saw that he seemed not to have much to do a good deal of the time – apparently he did his photographing mainly on trips. I rarely saw him with a camera, though he had shown contact sheets of his previous summer's work – a trip to Nova Scotia of perhaps two weeks' length – to my class. I was confused by his performance as a teacher, puzzled by his activity, or lack of it, as an artist, but also excited by what I was seeing of his previous work, and frankly fascinated by what – and how much – I was seeing of him.

At his suggestion I had begun to address him as Walker. Walker Evans III introduced himself to strangers as Evans, I had noticed, and he had referred to himself in writing once or twice in the third person, also as Evans. I had met no one, however, who called him Evans or Mr. Evans. He told me with noticeable pride that he had been given a name that did not readily suggest a nickname or abbreviation. 'Walk Evans' appeared on his name-tag in the photograph he showed me of his 50th reunion at Andover, but he said that name was never applied to him as a student. He had escaped the tags common among men of his generation such as Bunny (Edmund Wilson's boyhood nickname, which followed him to school and even after) and Cal (Robert Lowell's, short for Caliban), as well as the standard form of prepschool nickname: first syllable of the last name with a diminutive ending, which would have made him Evvie or Evsie. At Yale everyone, including secretaries and undergradates, called him Walker.

He usually called me Jerry (not a nickname but the given name that appears on my Texas birth certificate), which he sometimes spelled Jere when writing. I was called Thompson when he assumed his mock-pompous, pontificating voice (as in "Thompson will be remembered in the history of twentieth-century photography as..."), and some flattering epithet when he couldn't call up my actual name. At a reception he introduced me to an acquaintance by saying, "My old friend, you know this young genius, don't you?"

When he said Jerry, he pronounced the *y* more like a long *a* than the long *e* sounded by me and most other people. I think the diminutive was displeasing to his ear, so he turned it into something else. In a similar transmogrification, he remembered some polysyllabic names in his own particular way. A man he saw named Rothenberg he frequently called Rothmere in my hearing, and Trachtenberg usually became Trac. My course-mate Melinda Blauvelt became for him Bluey, a triple pun – on the first syllable of her name, of course; on the fact that she had been an undergraduate at Yale (in the first class to admit women and among the first of her sex to qualify for the standard old-boy nickname) and was therefore an old Blue; and finally because of her (he liked to insist) blue blood. (He understood her name to be of old Dutch origin.) This rechristening was not a semiconscious slip of the brain but a deliberate, arch, linguistic construction, a *bon mot*. Walker was quite proud of it.

The opening of the Yale show took place on 9 December 1971. I went to the reception with my own friends and so missed the official dinner and my first chance to see Walker in the role of honored celebrity. Isabelle and Hilton Kramer, then art critic of *The New York Times*, both came from New York for the opening, and Cleanth Brooks, the distinguished literary critic then on the Yale faculty, attended – which pleased Walker. I quickly learned that he liked his work to be appreciated beyond the insular world of photography and photographers.

In some ways "Walker Evans: Forty Years" was a concentrated version of the retrospective mounted earlier in the year by the Museum of Modern Art and still on national tour. The Yale show presented about ninety prints, the earliest dated 1928 (*Couple at Coney Island*), and the most recent, eleven prints in all, from 1971. The show filled the Yale Art Gallery's ground-floor west room, at that time the principal space for temporary exhibitions.

The entrance to the west gallery led a viewer into a large room hung with a single row of photographs. Movable walls broke up the room somewhat and provided additional space for hanging pictures. One of these walls stood to the right of the entrance, blocking any view of the right side of the gallery space. The exhibition began on the viewer's left, as the first print in the sequence made clear: it was a straightforward picture of a sign, the painted rendering of a large hand with a pointing index finger (Sandusky, Ohio, dated 1935). The finger pointed in the direction the viewer was to take in viewing the exhibition.

The photographs were not arranged in strict chronological order, but rather sequenced so that the form or subject of each picture was related in some way to the picture following it. There was, however, a general progression from early to recent: the newest pictures came mostly toward the end of the sequence orchestrated by Walker and Melinda.

Each photograph was trimmed and mounted on white board – most boards were 15 x 18 verticals, and the mounted prints were held onto the walls by sheets of glass and metal hooks. There were no frames. "So many frames to buy," I heard one Madison Avenue dealer complain when asked (about this time) why he had so few photography shows. And, he continued, you had to re-do the walls after the show because of all the nail holes.

I have been told that sales in artist's prints – lithographs, etchings, and engravings – boomed about the time that the price of a typical painting rose beyond the easy reach of a typical collector. About 1975 a similar boom began in the sales of photographs, but that boom came too late to benefit Evans. In 1971, even a museum with standards as high as those of the Yale Art Gallery – a museum that exhibited on its upper floors such candidates for the standard histories as Van Gogh's *Night Café* and Duchamp's *The Large Glass* – might consider extravagant the prospect of buying frames costing perhaps $20 apiece for prints that sold for about $100 each.

Even without frames, however, the small (I think none was larger than 11 x 14 inches) black-and-white photographic prints offered a dense, rich view of Evans's work. And, as the viewer wended his way around the room toward the area weighted with the most recent work, a surprise lay in store: beyond the concealing wall to the right of the entrance was a group of ten framed found objects, old rusted or faded roadside signs similar to those that appeared in a good number of the photographs on display. One of the signs on the wall – a large NEHI beverage sign – appeared in one of the exhibited photographs, a view of small-town Alabama buildings made in 1936 and reproduced in *Let Us Now Praise Famous Men*, the collaboration with James Agee that remains Evans's best-known book. Some kind of advertisement, billboard, or other sign was the principal subject-matter in a full third of the photographs in the exhibition.

Roadside signs installed in the Yale Art Gallery for the exhibition "Walker Evans: Forty Years," 1971–72

In his review for *The New York Times* Hilton Kramer said that, by hanging actual objects in the same gallery as his justly famous photographs of similar objects, Evans had "sprung a beguiling intellectual trap that estheticians will be extricating themselves from for years to come." Theorists and some artists did in fact begin (about five years later) worrying almost non-stop about the relationship, if any, between a photograph and objects appearing in the photograph. The phrase 'constructed realities' began to supplant such earlier key notions as 'decisive moment' and 'faithful witness.' But Kramer's prescient observation struck me at the time as enthusiastic hyperbole. I had no quarrel, however, with the review's headline assessment: "Second Evans Retrospective – Smaller but Powerful."

In addition to a beautiful large poster (showing a picture made in 1969 of a parlor stove), the Gallery printed a handsome checklist for the exhibition, a folder that held a carefully reproduced image of another stove, a cookstove photographed in 1971. Walker presented autographed copies of this checklist to friends and helpers. A favorite inscription ran:

To _____, from the small but powerful W.E.

Evans's *no trespassing* decrescendo installed in the Yale Art Gallery, 1971–72

AFTER THE SHOW opened there were still plenty of errands for me to run. Unused prints had to be returned to Old Lyme; negatives still at the Museum of Modern Art had to be fetched and returned to Evans's studio, and there always seemed to be something in Old Lyme that he wanted taken to the New York apartment, or vice versa. I had an aging Volkswagen bus that was useful for light transport. I realized that Walker was sorting out his and Isabelle's things, his coming to Old Lyme and hers, for the most part, going to New York. She was now visiting infrequently; within a year they would be divorced.

Where in all this activity the artist was I hadn't yet made out, but I was developing a growing admiration for the quality of Evans's mind, a mind startlingly unlike any I had admired, or known, before. My previous heroes had been scientists or scholars, and they displayed prodigious memories, vast bodies of organized knowledge, and other obviously impressive attainments. Walker knew a good deal, but it seemed to be all in pieces. I was shocked to suspect that he lacked what I would then have called an *overview* – a knack for deciding which organized body of knowledge could be connected to a particular question or fact. In school I had done a little research in libraries, and one effect of that experience had been to convince me that an easy familiarity with systematic knowledge was the hallmark of an educated mind. Walker seemed to ignore the main routes of learning that so impressed me then in favor of his own byways.

In speaking about the English Department at Yale he said, They're all critics, aren't they? They don't write literature – they're not artists, are they? as if he weren't quite sure, or perhaps

as if he thought they *should* be artists. And further:
You know, I believe Lionel Trilling is our best critic, don't you
think? Yes, I thought with the arrogance of my brief interrupted
graduate education, if you confine yourself to a rather dated,
humanistic, belle-lettristic sort of writing about literature, but
said only, "Walker, I think a number of younger critics have
developed new approaches and surpassed Trilling in subtlety
of analysis," to which he replied without interest, "Really?",
paused, regrouped, and went on to talk of other things.

He loved talk, even with someone as young and inexperienced
as I was. When I spent the night at Old Lyme (which by early
1972 was happening with increasing frequency), we often talked
late at night, a good time for him. He also listened, and seemed
genuinely interested in some, though certainly not all, of the
subjects I brought up. He was especially eager to hear or tell
how things worked. The thing might be a piece of equipment
or a travel route, but more likely a social ritual or an insider's
version of an historical event. He consistently directed his
energetic, fascinated, penetrating attention to subjects I had
heard discussed only in novels; full of animation, late at night,
stuttering briefly in search of a name or the right word, his
thumb rubbing rapidly in a circular motion against his
middle finger, he gave full display to his own particular brand
of brilliance.

He was steeped in the literature and culture of his young
manhood but seemed to me to be a man of his time, without any
real sense of history. D.H. Lawrence was real and vital to him; to
me at the time he seemed dated and unnecessary, the prophet of
a revolution that by 1970 had been fought and won. Shakespeare,
on the other hand, was to me a useful guide, an example whose
achievement remained the basis for understanding imagery and

character. To Walker he was someone who had written a long time ago. Walker might recall something he had heard Edmund Wilson say about Shakespeare, thus turning the conversation back to his own time. A young friend we both knew once lost the thread of some complicated story Walker was telling about Harry Hopkins, one of Roosevelt's New Dealers whom he had known in Washington in the mid-1930s. Pleading ignorance of the cast of characters, she said, Walker, I never spent much time in the study of American history. That's not history, he later said to me with some annoyance, That's my life!

Poetry interested him less, but fiction – fiction from about 1880 to World War II, even into the '50s and '60s – he knew well and discussed with enthusiasm, talking about writers whose names I had never heard before. He cited the example of Joyce, but I don't remember talking with him about specific passages, and I don't think he read Joyce while I knew him. During my time with him he read a good deal of biography and was especially interested in manners and style.

All his conversation was not so high-minded and literary as what I have reported so far might suggest, nor would transcripts of his daily conversation (had they been made) be published as readily by a university press as were those of Stieglitz, taken down by Herbert Seligman and published by Yale. The mind of Walker Evans, which I was coming to admire so, was often, as the Southern Methodists of my youth might have said, in the gutter. He liked to talk and joke about sex. This surprised me at first; I had imagined that the private conversation of a great artist might sound something like the letters of Keats. Evans's talk was often more like the Egyptian journals of Flaubert, with their randy banter about dancing girls and chancres. (He gave me a translation of these journals to read in 1973.)

He was interested in pornography, maintaining that it could be serious art if well done, which it almost never was. He read and recommended a magazine called *Penthouse Forum*. Its chief attraction was a column of readers' letters, which purported to ask or give advice but usually managed to describe in detail some inventive (hetero)sexual practice – letters carefully made up, Evans was sure, by the magazine's editors. Bernardo Bertolucci's movie *Last Tango in Paris*, he felt, was a triumph, a realistic treatment of relations between a man and a woman. He had been born a triple Scorpio, he explained, an astrological configuration said to favor two sets of organs, the eyes and the genitals.

The word 'genitals' once appeared in a letter he sent me, improbably dragged into his train of thought, spelled in such a way as to pun on either 'gentle' or 'gentile,' possibly on both. Wordplay and joking were also consistent features of his conversation, and it would be hard to say which he relished more, the opportunity to make a clever word joke or the chance to make a salacious reference (for an appropriate audience). In another note, ostensibly about travel plans, he refers in passing to dental work he has had done; this reference leads him to reflect that his mouth is now ready for all uses, legitimate or otherwise, which reflection leads to a denial of any improper intentions – a denial cast in the peculiar language of the Watergate hearings that filled the news that summer. This kind of wit – an improvised miniature version of the quicksilver segues of subject and context that direct the sequence of images in his book *American Photographs* – was a staple feature of his mental presence.

The curious man I was getting to know was hardly a teacher, much less a pedant, and not a moralist or reformer; he had no agenda or program for the world, not even the art world (though he wanted his place in it). A part of him, at least, was something I had not yet encountered: a man of the world, an Edwardian gentleman.

He was not a seeker of truth so much as a lover of paradox and irony, and a connoisseur of the *bon mot*. He admired form on the golf course at least as much as moral probity, and he was equally genuine in his heartfelt admiration of a well-crafted sentence (whatever it said) and a well-made English shirt, several of which he gave to me, along with good shoes and gray wool trousers, so that I might appear in company with him.

He was proud to be a Centurion and paid his Century Club dues before everything else except his mortgage. He was pleased to have enough French to petition the purser of the S.S. *France*, in writing, for a change of stateroom. He was elaborately courteous to almost everyone (I saw glaring exceptions a few times, usually deserved), yet he took sums of money for work he had little intention of doing, and endlessly delayed paying a well-known men's store for a fur coat he had bought on time. Slow pay, 'gentleman's C's,' and the imperfectly knotted tie were three of the gentlemanly attributes he explained to me, habits I had not previously known could be thought of as admirable. He once doubled his fee to a vulnerable editor – or rather, asked his young assistant (me) to phone the editor and double the fee – after an assignment had been delivered. Yet this same man, about the same time, lent that young assistant several hundred dollars to buy a used car without any clear idea of when he might get the money back. He readily handed over some large bills he kept (when he had them) filed under 'money' in the studio dictionary.

I struggled when describing this man to my other friends. Once, trying to explain him to a photographer who had not yet met him, I heard myself saying, "He's so covered with the dirt of the world!" He was worldly: an Anglophile, an admirer of

the aristock-o-rackacy (as he sometimes called them), a friend
of rich businessmen, a Time-Life editor, a ladies' man, a traveler
(preferably by ocean liner). He was interested in society's rituals
and manners, and involved in its snobberies (he explained to me
the derivation of the word 'snob'). He was worldly in a way that
a narrow-minded '60s college boy had not thought compatible
with intellectual substance. I can't remember what I supposed
Henry James (another Centurion) had been doing when not
writing. I thought artists were hermits who worked all the time.

I had expected Evans to be a good, straightforward,
conscientious worker, a diligent contributor to the great mass
of Truth accumulated in Art. I found instead a dandy, a courtier
whose behavior with women Stendhal would have recognized
and approved. He was brilliant, clever, vain, funny, often wicked,
charming, and usually a lot of fun to be around. His spirit was not
tidy, but it was large. As a close friend of his noted (in a carefully
worded observation), Walker was touched by greatness. Another
friend likened him to a flickering dynamo; still another called him
(in print) a devious giant.

He made pronouncements, sweeping statements that aspired
to sum up a broad area of thought or experience. These struck
me as spontaneous, rather than for effect; they just came to him
and popped out. Once during a classroom discussion of his
preferences in subject-matter, he came out with, "Prosperity
is my aesthetic enemy!" to his own amusement as much as the
students'. At Old Lyme he announced to me, apropos some of
his prints we were looking at, "The South is the only part of
this country where any real culture is to be found." After hearing
a Yale professor list several of Scott Fitzgerald's shortcomings
and failures, Evans answered by declaring that Fitzgerald was,
after all, an artist. For him, that fact silenced criticism.

I was especially struck by his penchant for summing up, because my own cast of mind favored the close examination of particular detail. I might be drawn to study the veination of some single leaf, but Evans would more likely want to characterize the forest. I loved the details in his work, but as I listened to and observed him more, I began to see why he had selected (or at least assented to) the epigraph from Matisse used in his book *Message from the Interior*: "L'exactitude n'est pas la vérité."

The synthetic habit of mind I observed was not the *overview*, the long perspective based on systematic knowledge, I had been surprised not to notice in him at once. Such an overview, as I understood it, involves a diligent effort to reconcile each long view, each broad conclusion, with every other long view. Evans took each epiphany, little or big, as it came. His intelligence was not like a steady searchlight; rather, it resembled so many separate flashes of lightning.

When I later watched him make photographs or edit his own pictures, I saw the same kind of mental operation at work. He didn't calculate or analyze, so far as I could tell; he just surveyed some arbitrarily defined body of data, scanning warily with his hooded eyes, and there it was!: some kind of synthesis – a good choice or preference, a conclusion, an answer, an epigram, a picture. I could analyze the process at length and explain to myself the logic of his choices and conclusions, but my analysis did not tell how the result was arrived at.

If others I had watched at work had impressed me with such qualities as memory, organization, and diligence, Evans stood out above all the rest in his ability to survey a random, apparently chaotic field of data and discern in it something significant and intelligible. To him the everyday world was an open book he knew how to read. I saw this ability first, and most clearly, in the pictures he made, pictures I was seeing more of as I got to know him better and spent more time in his house.

He was able to see automobiles, for example, so that their forms, in his pictures, while being immediate and convincing, managed at the same time to suggest something revealing about their essential quality as idea and element of social structure. This awareness of their significance crashed up against and played off architectural forms visible in some pictures, and landscape elements in others – collided with them with sufficient force to shoot off sparks of intellectual energy.

This energy has the quality of a barely contained explosion in the well-known view of Main Street, Saratoga Springs (1931). The automobiles in this picture, products of Henry Ford's lauded, still new, efficient assembly line, are stacked up in relentless uniformity, strongly outlined in their blackness against the rain-slicked street. Their phalanx drives a wedge between the two rows of façades lining the sides of the street, each row an anthology of textured, varied nineteenth-century building façades. In this view, in contrast to so many other views Evans made of nineteenth-century buildings, the façades are seen obliquely, rather than head on, and they are displaced towards the sidelines. The camera looks up the paved street, following, for the moment, the axis of movement of the black mechanical column. The camera eye looks on without insisting on a simply stated reaction or gloss as the elements of an evolving culture jocky for position, compete for the camera's attention. The flailing arms of barren elms, their branches dark against the white sky, preside overhead.

Spaced along the street and, larger, in the picture's lower left corner are streetlamps, appropriate ornaments for this scene: iron cast into floral forms, they are mechanical flowers carrying natural

Evans: *Main Street, Saratoga Springs*, 1931

gas from underground to supply artificial light at night to this civilized, cultivated, industrialized, dynamic landscape.

By early 1972 I was regularly printing for Walker and I studied the images as I worked. When printing the Saratoga glass-plate and similar negatives, I realized that everything had to show clearly. The more I looked, the more relevant data I saw, data inviting an attentive viewer to make connections. Printing Evans, I found, was not so much a question of getting some mysterious atmosphere, mood, or tone right; it was a question of making a clear print of his view, in this instance an ordinary – carefully managed, certainly, but ordinary, everyday, common (not Venice or Taos, not a battlefield, mountain, or sunset) – view of a small-town street. I have heard two serious, known photographers date their commitment to the medium to an encounter with this small-town view. It is clear, hard, allusive, authoritative – in Evans's own words, written about the time this picture was made, "*an open window staring straight down a stack of decades*."[1]

Discovering pictures on my own while looking through cardboard boxes full of prints in the studio or while trying to print the negatives was, I decided, preferable to listening to a professor explain them as I sat in class. Once or twice I told Walker what I was finding in his pictures. After one such session, during which I explained what I understood to be the logic connecting the several objects shown in one of his pictures, he responded by giving me the print I was talking about. You've earned it, he said, by explaining it to me. He showed no inclination to dispute or correct my explanation.

Evans seemed to be able to look at an unexceptional view of a small town or city and see its salient features, and the complex, tangled forces that had shaped it even when they worked at cross-purposes. The intelligibility he presented to the careful viewer of his pictures was not the same as the familiar patterns of analysis I had heard something about. Evans was not a Toynbeean or a Spenglerian or anything else that I could recognize. He seemed to get his understanding simply by looking clearly at the subjects that attracted him. He was not applying paradigms, but discovering connections. Obvious, almost inevitable, once you saw them in his pictures, the connections were harder to discern when you looked at an ordinary scene he had not yet photographed.

These connections were more immediate, local, eccentric, and less systematic than the conclusions of sociologists and historians I knew about. The scholars might speculate on causes, draw conclusions, or find patterns; Evans's pictures call attention to the key forces at work, illuminating them and balancing them delicately, so that a thoughtful viewer can look with interest time and again, coming away with a slightly different conclusion each time. Such a viewer might look at the Coney Island couple of 1928 and think about the nature of their tender contact with each other: the woman stooping so as to be shorter than the man, slightly, cautiously touching her dapper partner. Overhead floats a cartoon heart (moon, June).

Another time the same viewer might notice the same couple's shared experience of urban leisure, dressed up as they are, out of doors during the daytime on a hot, sunny day (Sunday? Holiday?). On still another viewing the couple might be seen to be in the thrall of the tacky finery that holds them motionless, looking in the hot sun, transfixed and passive before one of

the many forms of mass entertainment that appear in Evans's photographs: the movies, minstrel show posters, wild and exuberantly vulgar advertisements. Evans made art, as he would be the first to point out, not academic sociology: the pictures reflect on the presence of significant forces in a particular spot of historical time and enjoy playing them off against each other. His pictures do not drag the viewer to a final, unchangeable conclusion or a simply put message. Pictures by other photographers of similar subjects often do, but his don't.

Evans's perceptual talents, I learned, were not restricted to the views he made of American scenes. For several years at least he had been avidly collecting found objects and trash of all kinds to make into collages, or simply to frame and display. When I knew him he found a bit of hourglass-shaped crushed felt, a piece of trash that had been run over and impregnated with road grease so that it held its vaguely organic outline. He put it against a light blue paper outline and said, That's my mother, in a long dress and a bustle. Once he said it, it was hard to see the felt as resembling any other thing quite so much.

He made a few arrangements of beach trash to frame; when I assisted in this work he frequently asked for a thing by calling it his metaphorical name (body part) rather than its ordinary name (stick). We set aside firewood that forked into two branches of about equal thickness; these were torsos he might have a use for some day.

By early 1972 I was regularly looking through the mass of pictures in the studio. A print might be requested by his dealer, or perhaps a magazine, and I would search for it. Unless I could remember having seen the requested picture, and where, I had to look through all the prints in the room since there was no filing system to speak of.

After a few searches I began to look through his work on my own. When I stayed overnight at Old Lyme there were long slow mornings that were ideal for this. Gradually the power of his work, and something of the complexity of his relationship to the visible world, began to sink in. I had been attracted to his pictures from my first sight of them, but now, increasingly, I saw the subtlety, the allusiveness, the literate intelligence that made his pictures different from the work of other photographers I admired. I began to see how enormously complicated were his interest in and attachment to the things he photographed. I recall writing a letter to a friend one night while I was staying at Old Lyme, a letter that dwelt at length on the number of electrified kerosene lamps in the house, and on the prominence of these lamps in several Evans photographs from the South – notably in the picture showing a kerosene lamp on the oilcloth-covered kitchen table reproduced in *Let Us Now Praise Famous Men*.

By LATE WINTER of that year I had known Walker Evans for several months. I had worked on his exhibition, begun to spend time in his house and had had many opportunities to look at and think about his pictures, but I had not yet seen him at work as a photographer. The spring after the Yale show, in late March, we took a working trip together to the Eastern Shore of Virginia, where we were joined by Melinda Blauvelt for a few days. Finally I saw Evans photograph; he was working in what I might now call his old mode, using Rolleiflexes with black-and-white film, and seeking out mostly architectural subjects, some of which he had spotted several years earlier but never photographed. Earlier that year he had given me Wilmington, Delaware, as a gift – the city itself, not a picture of it. He said that the architecture was marvelous, and they permitted parking on only one side of the street at a time (leaving the other side uncluttered for the photographer's convenience), but he had never gotten around to working there himself. I could try it instead.

On this trip I drove and Evans directed. He led us to a pair of Victorian gingerbread outbuildings he had known about for a long time. They stood in a field, and Evans got out of the car to approach them with his camera, which he was using without a tripod. He made a sort of semicircle around the buildings, stopping briefly to make exposures as he walked. By this time I had looked through enough of his negatives to know that on occasion he made as many as ten or a doxen 8 x 10 negatives, and negatives of other sizes as well, of the same subject at nearly the same time. Why, I wondered, did he make so many?

Contact sheet of Evans's pictures of the *gingerbread twins*,
near Accomac, Virginia, 1972. Grease pencil markings on
three frames on top right are by Evans

Evans: *Virginia Eastern Shore*, 1972. A finished, cropped print as signed and exhibited by Evans

I developed and contact-printed the Virginia film, and the contact sheet today does not look as haphazard as I thought his shooting pattern was then. Far from looking frantic, it looks paced, controlled. There are three frontal views, fairly close, all with about the same framing and varying only in negative density – they are brackets, variations in exposure made to guarantee a properly exposed negative, one with densities that would yield a good print. There are three frontal views from slightly further off, also exposure brackets. Then there are three exposure brackets from an oblique angle – made from a position slightly off to the houses' right, with a road in the foreground. Finally there are three exposure brackets from closer up, from about the same angle of view but close enough to preclude a strip of road in the foreground. When the 12-exposure roll was finished, he stopped: a systematic, measured survey.

Three were marked by him on the contact sheet, the two frontal views and the closer oblique view. In all instances the whole negative area is outlined in orange grease pencil, but when I showed him enlarged prints he said he didn't want all that foreground. It must be cropped out, as he had assumed I would do. So the squares became horizontal rectangles, and their exact proportions seemed not to be critical; they were left up to me.

Later I decided that on this and a few other expeditions we made about this time, Evans was going through familiar motions with only mild interest. He was making pictures he wanted to make of subjects that interested him (that had interested him, in this instance, for years) but without the concentration and desire to wring every possible bit of meaning out of the details of light, framing, and perspective that characterize his best work. After I watched him working with real excitement, a little later, it seemed to me that, when doing this work, he had not been fully awake.

Walker had some color film with him in Virginia, and he talked a lot about the roadside signs we saw. On April Fool's Day, 1972, he found a shack in the middle of another Virginia field with a rusted Coca-Cola sign on it. The sign was so long that it extended from one side of the small shack to the other; its ends had been sheltered by the eaves of the roof and were less rusted than the rest of it. This detail delighted him, and he photographed the shack in black-and-white, with a Rolleiflex, and with 35mm color slide film, using a Leica. He also said he'd like to have the sign himself. Eventually two students collected it and took it to Old Lyme, where he photographed it again in his yard with color negative film. Then he had it installed high on the living room wall of his house. For a time a framed, signed color print of the slide he made on 1 April 1972 hung in the guest bedroom.

Exposure bracketing was something I knew about, but what kind of bracketing did this manifold appropriation (or arrogation, or thievery) represent? I thought of two separate views he had made in 1935 (apparently on the same day) of Belle Grove plantation – one with a large blackened stump in the foreground (ruin rising gaunt, etc.) and another from about the same angle, with a young sapling in the foreground (hope springs eternal...). Restless, it occurred to me, was a word that might be used to describe the mind of Walker Evans.

Evans: untitled [Coca-Cola shed in Accomac Country,
Virginia, between Locustville and Wachapreague],
April 1, 1972 (black-and-white)

EVANS WAS REGULARLY collecting, or commissioning the collecting of roadside and other kinds of signs by late 1972. He was still photographing them *in situ*, but he was also photographing them, or causing them to be photographed, at home, often in the yard or nailed to the side of his house.

One afternoon in the late winter of 1972 he and I took three recent finds (or gifts) out into the yard at Old Lyme to photograph in black-and-white. ONE/WAY/[arrow], metal, whose arrow points to the one edge of the sign that is rusted to a ragged fringe, was nailed onto the neat vertical boards of house siding, while NO HUNTING/ ALLOWED, paper on wooden board, and ...T.../ BY PERMISSION ONLY, paper attached to wooden board with nails through bottlecaps, were nailed to trees in the yard. I then set up the 4 x 5 view camera I was using at the time. Walker told me not to make too much of a picture, but just to close in on each sign. He went inside while I fussed with the camera, but he insisted I call him out to press the shutter release.

He signed the mounted prints which resulted from that afternoon's work, and at the time I understood that in doing this he was not only saving himself effort but also making a point about what part of the process involved authorship, though neither he nor I used that word then. Later, after helping him fill a number of print orders, I came to think that he was having a little fun with the notion of 'vintage print,' a notion that was beoming current among collectors and dealers. A year or two after Evans's death I saw one of these yard pictures of signs, which I had printed on a warm-toned printing paper, offered for sale in a gallery as a vintage print. Walker would have been amused.

Home photograph
commissioned, directed,
and signed by Evans

Home photograph
commissioned, directed,
and signed by Evans

'Vintage,' applied to photographic prints, refers to prints made
by the photographer around the time the negative was made. The
justification for this distinction is the belief that photographers,
when negatives are new, are best able to concentrate with
enthusiasm on the fine details of printing and have access to the
materials they were accustomed to using at the time they made
the negatives. Thus, the thinking goes, they are able to produce
a print more expressive of their original intentions (which would
still be fresh in their minds), and therefore superior to any print
they or some assistant might make at any later time.

This theory is reasonable, but it assumes that all photographers
are paying perfect attention when making the first prints from a
negative, and that they carefully destroy all early attempts that

Home photograph
commissioned, directed,
and signed by Evans

don't measure up. It also assumes that photographers organize their prints in such a way that they can later tell with certainty which prints were made at which time. Otherwise collectors have only their connoisseurship, or that of a dealer, to rely on. Such connoisseurship is pretty hard to come by – it involves looking at numerous prints made over time from each of many negatives, as well as a detailed knowledge of both the history of photographic materials and the history of the photographer in question. Further, such connoisseurship is dangerously intertwined with economics: it is to the advantage of the dealer to have an old, datable collectible to sell (even if its survival is a mere historical accident), and to the advantage of the collector to have a 'definitive print' (a notion that is cousin or closer to the current favorite cliché of popular journalism, the 'defining moment'). The word 'rare' hovers in the background, but some negatives are printed dozens of times. Which prints are rare – the ones that are most expressive? The ones with cryptic notations on the back? The ones that happen to be in commerce at a particular moment?

Walker was troubled by the notion of the vintage print. When I helped him fill orders he shied away from prints that were discolored or distressed; he felt that they impeached his standards of craft. He also told me he didn't always know which prints were printed when, and he disliked being pressured, or tempted, to attest to the age of a particular piece of paper. The benchmark guides for his work, it is widely thought, are prints that had been out of his hands for a long time, but were those always the prints he thought best, even at the time? He told me that Lincoln Kirstein had taken prints "from my wastebasket," as he put it, and given them to a museum. (I think he said it was the Metropolitan.) The prints were discolored in a way that displeased Walker. He said he had tried to give the museum good, new prints in exchange for the Kirstein gift, but that the museum had not agreed with him.

When I worked in the studio very few of the prints I saw were well organized. He had made up small packets of tiny contact prints from some of his earliest rollfilm (not 35mm) pictures. I recall that there were several prints from each negative, that they looked fairly consistent, and that all the prints from each negative were stored together in a single envelope. I thought that in this early work Walker seemed to be making small unnumbered editions of some of his favorite pictures, though we never discussed this. I can't be sure now that in 1972 or '73 I had ever heard the word 'edition' applied to photographic prints.

The only other evidence of organization I recall was a metal box or two containing file folders numbered to correspond to the plate numbers of *American Photographs*. This file had been set up at some past time and contained a number (but not a complete set) of prints.

Walker would quickly and decisively distinguish between a *good* and a *bad* print. *That* one should be stronger, he might say, or (of a picture showing a church organ), You can read the sheet music in a good print. But further than this he was reluctant to go, when I knew him. He had used assistant printers for years, and he was genuinely troubled when Da Capo Press published detailed ordering instructions for his Farm Security Administration work. He had been a federal employee during 1935 and 1936, and many of his negatives from those years were on file in the Library of Congress, which supplied prints to anyone for a small fee. Walker felt that such a print, made by a photoduplication service, might somehow compete with a print from his collection, sold over his signature.

He was more concerned about how a print was mounted than about when it had been made. Dry mounting (fusing the print to a paper board by means of a heat-activated adhesive tissue) was falling out of favor among collectors, who wanted prints hinged into overmats as other kinds of art prints were. ('Archival' was another new word coming into wide use among dealers and collectors.) Walker wondered whether we might salvage some good prints that had been dry mounted. We experimented by taking a couple of old prints mounted in this way – he suggested trying some yellowed ones in case the experiment failed – and soaking them in water for a few days. Then, under his direction, I tried to peel the softened print off the board – separating it from an early signature in the process. The prints came apart, and we lost both the rare prints and the early signatures. Walker didn't mind the loss; he wouldn't have wanted to show or sell those prints in any event.

He resolved from then on to have prints mounted by hinging them into overmats. When a request came in, I looked through the studio to see whether I could find a print he thought was good. If I found one, he had it mounted and sent it off at the same price, whether it was an overrun from the recent Museum of Modern Art printing (done mostly by Jim Dow), a Museum of Modern Art proof print made during the selection process for the 1971 show by the museum's darkroom staff, a test print for the 1971 Ives-Sillman portfolio (made by a team directed by Thom Brown), or an older print from some previous time that happened to be available. If no good print could be found, I'd try to find the negative and make one.

Some negatives could not be found, but Walker was vague about what might have happened to them. We never could find the view of the License Photo Studio (the first picture in

American Photographs) with the swinging sign unblurred, only
the second negative, which shows the sign in motion. So I printed
that one instead. Five or six negatives had to be borrowed back
from the Library of Congress. After printing, they somehow got
lost in the studio for a few months, but they were finally found
and returned.

I worked in Walker's darkroom, a small room in a corner of
the studio with black walls and ceiling. He had a sink and a small
working surface along one wall, and, at right angles to this
counter, a surface holding two enlargers, an Omega C-2 (which
took negatives up to $3\frac{1}{4}$ x $4\frac{1}{4}$, I think – I know it was too small to
take 4 x 5 negatives) and a Leitz Focomat for 35mm negatives.
I printed the larger negatives in a simple wooden contact printing
frame, one of the enlargers serving as the light source. If I
printed on Kodak Azo, a slow-speed contact printing paper, I took
the head of the Focomat apart to expose the bare bulb. The only
other paper I used in that darkroom was a faster-speed enlarging
paper, Kodak Polycontrast. When printing on this paper I used
light directed through one of the enlargers.

I began with arcane print developers such as Amidol, and I
printed the first negative assigned me too dark deliberately so
that I could bleach out the highlights and produce a more brilliant
print. Walker was not impressed. He didn't think the print color
produced by Amidol was worth the trouble and expense, and the
bleaching seemed to him an unnecessary extra step. I began to
use store-bought Dektol and made prints that could be sent off
as soon as they were dry.

The darkroom was too small to hold both of us, so I would
make test prints until I thought I might be close and then show
him what I was doing. He would say something like, A little
lighter, or perhaps, A bit stronger (his way of asking for more

contrast), and I would make the needed adjustment: switch to another paper contrast grade, alter the printing exposure, or perhaps change the developing time of the print. Some of the negatives (for example, the only surviving one of *Penny Picture Display, Savannah*) are of uneven density and require a number of dodging and burning-in procedures to get a print of uniform quality. When complex hand movements shade the printing light, causing different amounts of light to fall on different parts of the image, no two prints from the negative are ever exactly alike.

I recall working on the *Penny Picture Display* print for what must have seemed too long for Walker. He came to the darkroom door to ask how I was doing. I was struggling with the hand movements needed to achieve the evenness I wanted, and since every print looked a little different I was continuing until I had two or three that were pretty much the same so I could show them to him. He looked in and saw the wash tray with what might have been fifteen or twenty sheets of paper in it, all the same picture. He said, Hey man, that's enough: this looks fine! He also said something about wasting paper in pursuit of the perfect print. I told him I guessed I had a few that would do, and he instructed me to save all the ones I had in the wash. After the prints were dry I separated the ones I thought were best, but I never tore the rest up, and I don't remember how, or for how long, my selection might have stayed intact. I recently saw one of my rejects in a New York gallery.

After a few printing sessions Walker came to trust my judgment. He always reviewed the finished prints, but he didn't come into the darkroom so often to watch work in progress. Later I sometimes had to take negatives away – the 4 x 5s, for instance – to print, and then he didn't see the results until they were finished and dry, ready for his signature.

Evans was selling these prints from time to time, both through his dealer Robert Schoelkopf and directly, but not in large numbers. I can't remember his selling a print for more than $150, and I don't recall ever being asked to hunt up an old print rather than a recently made one. If I could find any good print, that was what he sold.

When he sold prints in quantity, the price dropped. A student friend arranged for him to sell twelve or fifteen prints to a Harvard student she knew for a round $100 a print, and the prints were delivered in overmats paid for by Evans. He was so pleased with this deal that he drove to Boston (on 27 May, 1972) to deliver the prints in person. (The buyer received him for lunch in a private room at Locke-Ober, the traditional and popular Boston restaurant.)

Later, near the end of his life, he made several large deals. In one I remember (in the spring of 1974), he got $10,000 for a large number of prints, but his per-print price, as far as I knew, never topped $150. His last deal was for an even larger round sum, but it set no per-print records – not on the high side, at any rate.

He had a small bank balance – I remember celebration when he banked the $10,000; he said that never in his life did he think he would have so much money in the bank. But mostly, until the last sale, he managed to stay financially a little ahead (or not too far behind) during the time I knew him. His print sales were a help, but far from a living. He had a small pension from Time-Life, but until the last few months of his life he thought of himself as a working man, one who rarely turned down the offer of a paying job.

At this time, dinner at the Old Heidelberg in New Haven would have cost $10 or $12 for two – he rarely dined alone and usually picked up the tab for a younger dinner partner. A

Turnbull and Asser shirt from London cost $27, and the car he drove, a Chevy Vega station wagon, had cost no more than $3,000. His mortgage was $200-something a month, if I remember correctly.

These considerations are not out of place in an account of the man who, when he sat on his one PhD oral examination board, asked just one question. The candidate had written on Alfred Stieglitz, and Evans's only question, he told me, was whether the candidate knew how Stieglitz got his money. Stieglitz had a private cash income all his life, Walker said to me, and he wanted to be sure the young scholar knew it.

FILLING REQUESTS for prints of his older, well-known pictures occupied some of Walker's attention in 1972, but I discovered he was most interested in working with signs – photographing them in the field, collecting them, and photographing them again at home. His earlier pictures of signs often showed them in some kind of context: the NEHI sign in a middle distance view of brick buildings in Alabama, or the painting of vegetables that is part of the collage of signs on the porch of the South Carolina Art School ("General Lafayette Spoke From This Balcony"). These signs were often permanently attached to their settings, painted directly onto the bricks or boards of the buildings they embellished. In pictures like these, the individual signs are only a part of the larger visual and intellectual construct, so to speak, of the photograph. Each sign is only one element of the picture, and the largest meaning of the picture results from Walker's deliberate combination of all the elements in the view.

The signs he was seeking out when I knew him were often less referential, more self-contained, less dependent on context – indeed, most of them were portable. They tended to be condensed poems, or at least jokes. NO TRESPASSING is invaded by a splotch of corrosion entering from its perimeter; a school crossing sign from some distant, long-past time is a kind of vernacular Grecian urn, showing still-young children fading into an oblivion of rust. These signs contain their own meanings, and their own ironies, independent of Walker's shaping. He did not construct or modify their meanings; he confined his role to selecting (along with, of course, removing the sign from one context – its functional one – to place it into another, that of the gallery/museum collection). Significantly, he favored the word 'lifting,' which implies elevation as well as removal, to describe this activity. In an artistic gesture that takes ironic understatement to its furthest reach, he even experimented with framing and showing the signs themselves, rather than his photographs of them.

A number of these new signs were given to Walker; he never saw or knew their original locations. In general, these signs, and their significance, are smaller, more intimate than the pictures he had made of signs earlier. They are complete in themselves, often devoid of historical reference beyond noting the mere passage of time, and oblivious of any but the most general awareness of society and its patterns. If a number of the earlier pictures of signs had seemed, by merely documenting, to comprehend such large, complex historical structures as to be epic, these newer discoveries were clearly lyrical, more personal. Often he was interested in the simple beauty of his finds, in their soft faded colors and weathered textures. They delighted him, and he wanted to have them.

Walker himself described this new interest in words perhaps more florid but no less precise than his "*open window staring straight down a stack of decades*" of forty years earlier. These words were written for the wall panel in his Yale show of 1971–72 when he exhibited framed signs along with his photographs. This formulation, like his earlier one, invites a close, careful reading:

The installation, here, of actual graphic "found objects" may need little or no interpretation via the written word. Assuredly, these objects may be felt – experienced – in this gallery, by anyone, just as the photographer felt them in the field, on location. The direct, instinctive, bemused sensuality of the eye is what is in play – here, there, now, then.

A distinct point, though, is made in the lifting of these objects from their original settings. The point is that lifting is, in the raw, exactly what the photographer is doing with his machine, the camera, anyway, always. The photographer, the artist, "takes" a picture, symbolically he lifts an object or combination of objects, and in so doing he makes a claim for that object or that composition, and a claim for his act of seeing in the first place. The claim is that he has rendered his object in some way transcendent, and that in each instance his vision has penetrating validity.

In his eagerness to stress the importance of 'lifting,' Walker oddly compresses 'object' and 'combination of objects,' ignoring what seems to me now a crucial distinction, a distinction that explains why I think his earlier pictures are larger in ambition and meaning than the home photographs of single signs, isolated from setting, and his framed presentation of the single signs themselves. But Walker wasn't thinking about his earlier pictures when he wrote this statement, nor would his temperament (with its lack of interest in *overview*) lead him to compare recent pictures with earlier photographs of similar subject. Several times I heard him wonder aloud why people always asked about his work from several decades ago; Why, he asked, didn't they want to know about what he was doing *now*? And what he was doing now (in 1972), as the Yale label makes clear, often involved a direct attraction, relatively uncomplicated by ironic overtones, to objects that pleased him. In spite of whatever echoes he may have heard of earlier work with similar subjects, the bemused, sensual eye of Walker Evans was frequently drawn to objects he found simply beautiful. Not unlike, I though at the time, his attraction to the graceful kerosene lamps that filled the house in Old Lyme.

It seems to me that, at this point in his work, Walker had identified a new subject area of great interest to him, and had begun to zero in on it – he was an active collector, and he was photographing the signs that attracted him then almost to the exclusion of everything else – but was not yet sure, exactly, how to use this pared-down version of a familiar subject to full effect. I was puzzled then, and as I look now at some of the home pictures and at pictures of the signs themselves, it seems to me that they aren't quite good enough for Walker Evans. In spite of the claim he makes in the Yale wall label, the signs themselves, for all their beauty and interest, are not as compelling as the complex use his earlier pictures had made of other signs. His attraction is clear, but some important, necessary elements – elements neither of us could have identified in 1972 – are lacking.

IN NOVEMBER 1972, all artistic work stopped because Walker became seriously ill. He was at Dartmouth College for a semester as artist-in-residence, where he had been spending a little time driving around photographing farmhouses and churches (old mode), and more time photographing and especially collecting signs, which he arranged to have framed in the well-appointed woodshop of the Hopkins Center at Dartmouth. By early November he found it difficult to climb a single flight of stairs; he felt so weak that he consulted a doctor, who immediately checked him into Mary Hitchcock Hospital in Hanover. The examination disclosed a bleeding ulcer, the same nemesis that had put him out of action in the early 1960s.

Later in the month, he underwent abdominal surgery, which removed what was left of his stomach from the '60s and fashioned a pouch-like substitute from the upper part of his small intestine. The operation was serious enough to make him revise his will beforehand. He included among his heirs a young artist and photographer about my age named Virginia Hubbard. Though she lived at some distance from Walker – I don't remember exactly where – she had been a close friend since the late '60s, and they had gone on working trips together. She had been an early, enthusiastic collaborator in sign-lifting.

Walker's complex surgery entailed a long, difficult recovery that kept him more or less invalid until the following March. In mid-January I took him home from the hospital to Old Lyme where I moved in to live and, with the help of Charlee Brodsky, a hard-working friend who visited several days a week, to manage his household affairs until he got back on his feet.

Evans in his Old Lyme
bedroom during his
convalescence,
February, 1973

At first Walker was quite weak and in frequent need of strong painkillers, including Demerol, that kept him in a fog. Gradually he healed, was able to eat more easily, and his strength began to return. In addition to helping manage the household Charlee introduced Walker to pot roast (using a cup as dipper, he drank the juice directly from the cooking pot as a fortifying cocktail), and she periodically supplied companionship that was a welcome break from the steady dose of mine he was getting. I was keeping track of his checkbook at the time, and I paid us each a small weekly salary for six or eight weeks. I was going into New Haven only one day a week, so my opportunity for doing the small photographic jobs that were an important part of my income was limited.

During that period Walker did no work of any kind; in the beginning he was barely awake for days at a stretch. But as he recovered and his strength returned, he forced himself to read, using his index finger to keep his eyes moving across the page in a straight line. As soon as he was able, he began to go on daily outings (when the weather permitted, he walked the beach at Old Black Point, usually bringing back a few bits of beach trash, which interested him almost as much as signs), and by late February he was well enough to write for publication. Lee Friedlander commissioned an introduction for a portfolio of his own pictures, which Walker polished until he was pleased with it.

By March he was able to visit friends in the Caribbean, and when he returned he could live more or less on his own. Along the way he had had a taste of psychotherapy, suggested by friends

Evans walking on the
beach at Old Black Point
(near Niantic, CT),
February, 1973

because of the malaise (depression? Walker insisted on the word melancholy) that had accompanied his long, sometimes frustrating recovery at home. Also he had an exhibition in New York: his dealer, Robert Schoelkopf, scheduled an April show on short notice to give him an opportunity to sell some prints and help offset the expenses of his illness. Many negatives had to be printed for the show, and this preparation was my most concentrated period of printing for him. Some of the negatives we had 'found' together, dug out of this or that hiding place in the studio during the organizing sessions that were one form of occupational therapy I tried to introduce during the long winter of his recovery. Another was taping sessions, during which Walker and I would talk about whatever came into his head (use of the words 'hopefully' and 'none', my past, Georgia O'Keeffe's breasts, etc.). We also used a newly acquired School of Art 8 x 10 enlarger to try some modest enlargements of his 8 x 10 negatives. There were several 11 x 14, and one or two 16 x 20 enlargements from well-known negatives offered for sale in Schoelkopf's front room. The 8 x 10s were listed at $150 and the 16 x 20s at $400. None of the latter was sold.

Ten or a dozen of the 8 x 10s sold, though, and the show was a bracing, upbeat experience. Walker treated himself to lunch at the expensive fish restaurant Gloucester House before the opening reception, and a small group went with him to a French restaurant that evening. He was in fine form and looked splendid with a dark tan and a new, full, snow-white beard, begun during his hospital stay.

His mood that spring was generally celebratory. He even celebrated my graduation (with an MFA degree) from Yale. On three separate occasions, he gave me three different graduation presents, all books. One, a paperback edition of

Picasso's sculpture, is dated "Graduation Day, 1973" in the same pen that scratched out the (discounted) price. Another was the two-volume small-print edition of the Oxford English Dictionary, which cost $75 – a good sum in 1973, especially for a man who later that year would have to borrow the money to pay for wine and flowers at his own seventieth birthday party. The third gift was John Szarkowski's *Looking at Photographs*, with the following inscription:

Instead of the conventional graduation present of the full-calf bound copy of "A Woman of Pleasure", I bequeath you this volume of John's thoughts + sights. I couldn't get "Fanny Hill". Yrs heartily,
Walker
June 1973

The living room in Old Lyme, January or February, 1973. A finished, framed collage leans against one of Evans's largest beachcombing finds. The stockinged foot belongs to W E

Walker *was* hearty in June 1973: he was in good health, for him, after having nearly died; he had made some sales and had a little money in the bank, instead of just a pile of debts; and he was in demand for college lectures. One morning that spring, as he walked out of his bedroom at Old Lyme, he announced (one of his sweeping judgments) that he was on his last lap around the track; he intended to make it a good one.

APART FROM HIS beachcombing and other collecting – he thought of his finds as raw material for serious collages, among other things – he hadn't done much artistic work since the previous autumn in Hanover. In the summer of 1973, though, he found out about a new camera that interested him, the Polaroid SX-70. This was a streamlined modern-looking apparatus that collapsed into a neat flat block of leather-covered chrome when not in use. It yielded a square picture, like the Rolleiflexes, but the viewfinder was very bright, easy to look through at eye level (even while wearing glasses), and its image was not reversed left to right as that of the Rolleiflex was. The user could focus continuously, without attachments and with an accurate viewfinder image, from infinity down to a distance of about one foot. Also, the Polaroid gave finished pictures fully developed in a few minutes, just after they came out of the camera. And they were in color.

Evans put off trying this camera for a time, but once he started he worked steadily. Almost at once he began work on all the major subjects that would occupy him for the rest of his working life: signs, debris on the street, architectural curiosities, and the faces of friends and strangers. The ease of viewing, the freedom to move as close as he wanted without adjustments or difficulty, and the instant processing – the sudden availability of all these attractive features led him to an explosion of photographic activity. I first saw his new photographic mode in action shortly after his return from England, where he must have hit his stride.

A few weeks after Walker returned from his trip in the fall of 1973, he was scheduled to lead a Yale student workshop to

Virginia, and I was to go along as his faculty assistant. The destination was his choice – the Whispering Pines Motel, in Accomac on the Eastern Shore, the same place where we had stayed two springs before. He and a dozen or so advanced students would all work on the same subject, ot at least in the same area, one of interest to him and presumably to them as well, and then discuss their common experience in a follow-up critique session. The prospect of working in the field alongside Walker Evans, it was thought, would be of great interest to photography students at Yale.

The trip got off to a difficult start. Walker always had trouble, when I knew him, getting out of the house before afternoon. He would wake up, have breakfast, go back to bed, get up again, then go about the business of getting dressed. He encountered numerous distractions on the way to getting ready for the day.

This particular day – Tuesday, 16 October 1973 – he had to meet the students in New Haven, pick up his pay (important), and then make it to Cape May, New Jersey, for the first night's stay. The next day they would take the ferry to Lewes in Delaware and drive on to Accomac for a stay of several days.

I was to drive with Walker in his car, the students in several other cars. As we prepared to leave Old Lyme I was watching the clock, since the drive from New Haven to Cape May would take at least four or five hours, and we had to get to New Haven first. Eventually we made it to the School of Art, met the students, got his check, and headed out for Cape May. Somewhere along the way Walker realized that in our rush one of us had neglected to load the bag containing his clothes and, more important, his medications. These included Tofranil, a daily antidepressant carefully rationed out to him by his psychiatrist.

Going back to Old Lyme was not possible, so Walker decided to telephone doctors and pharmacists from the motel in Cape May to arrange for replacement prescriptions. He would pick up some clothes along the way, which, with the telephone, doctor, and pharmacy bills, would no doubt account for a good part of the $1,000 he was being paid to lead the week-long workshop.

Telephoning took a good part of the next morning, which was cool and sunny. Some time around noon Walker finally emerged into the sunlit day, his medications under control, a morning meal in his new stomach, carrying his new camera and a supply of film.

He began to work almost at once. We were walking near the car in a vacant lot, and for a time everything he spotted seemed to be something he had been after for years. A discarded six-pack harness, seen from directly above against the fading fall grass and carefully squared in the frame, became in his picture a singular talismanic rune, or perhaps a brassiere for a pig. He made picture after picture of this and other finds, bending over to photograph, walking a few steps, and then bending over again. Sometimes he made several exposures of one object, not waiting for the individual prints to develop but letting them accumulate at the exit slot of the camera or whisking them into the side pocket of his jacket without glancing at the nascent image.

The things shown in some of these pictures seemed flattened onto the picture ground because the camera is carefully held directly over them. In several instances – pictures of beverage or other cans – the object has been literally flattened; its foreshortened image is the result not of perspective and point of view but rather the weight of the automobile that passed over it.

These 'object portraits' recall other Evans pictures, such as the kitchen implements on the wall of the Alabama tenant farmer's kitchen, and more particularly the common tools photographed for a *Fortune* essay. The earlier pictures, though, are severe, whereas these later ones are whimsical, even funny – they show trash viewed as treasure – and their bright colors enhance their charm. These pictures consistently display wit – Walker often used the word in its French sense, meaning liveliness of mind, rather than in its more sober eighteenth-century English sense, meaning understanding. In using his camera to make these pictures, Walker turned a quotidian chore, the few labored steps from eating-place to car, into an expedition of discovery, a small trek for a cultivated eye in an aging body.

Wit is a quality of mind frequently enlisted to make the most of a difficult situation. If there is one feature of the Walker Evans I knew that is central to his character and life at this time, it is his reliance on and pervasive use of wit, in this sense. It permeated every aspect of his experience, even his grimmest, appearing in the most unlikely situations. His physical frailty was noticeable when I first met him; by the end of his active life it was almost preposterous that so frail a man, a walking scarecrow, could get through the day, let alone dress up, flirt, and work productively. Throughout this sometimes painful late journey, Evans's liveliness of mind persistently raised the tone, until very near the end.

Nor was this resilient enforced wit a response only to his declining physical powers. This condition, physical weakness, was but a concentrated immediate example of a more generalized condition – call it the human condition, or perhaps the dilemma of the artist-genius in an alien culture. (Lawrence, Baudelaire, Flaubert, Joyce – what genius of modern times ever found his culture up to his requirements?) Whether discovered in decorations made from newspapers and printed ads arranged in a rude shack or among the refined selections of a cultivated, even

Mandarin eye – bits of bright trash pulled from a culture's huge rubbish heap – making the best of a bad situation extended into Evans's thought and work far beyond accommodating his stiff legs and failing strength.

The pictures of trash Walker made in Cape May and elsewhere offer many pleasures to the sensual eye, but beneath their bright surface runs a deeper current, a strong one that runs through much of his work, early and late. Many of his parking lot pictures are of things carelessly dropped or deliberately discarded. Photographing these humble cast-offs is the exact opposite of photographing the official ornaments of dominant culture, Park Avenue skyscrapers or Hoover Dam. Evans had always tended to ignore the large new official building in the courthouse square to poke around the neglected quarters of a town. It was usually in out-of-the-way places that he made his richest finds; this habit suggests some doubt that the official guide book will lead to the things of true importance produced by this culture. The Coca-Cola corporate headquarters, and its balance-sheet, might interest the readers and some editors of *Fortune* magazine, but not Evans. His interest was in the discarded pull-top from a Coca-Cola can, or the odd flattened can itself, and the rusted signs the company had abandoned long ago. He was not interested in the achievement of record, but the incidental detritus. It is only by accident, or through the agency of erratic genius, that true worth is found, and it is often found among the accidental cast-offs of established culture.[2]

Small wonder that the organized professor, the purveyor of accepted knowledge, was so hard to find in Walker. It was not in him, and he was deeply suspicious of the whole business. Instead of explaining, he preferred to photograph trash in the gutter, sign and frame the picture, and arrange to have it exhibited on a

Evans: *Joe's Auto Graveyard, Pennsylvania*, 1936
(actual date is 1935, according to Resettlement
Administration field notes I consulted in 1982)

prestigious wall: What d'ya make of that? A gesture not so different, when I come to think of it, from the picture he made in 1935 of Joe's auto graveyard, a dryly wicked mock landscape which deflates Henry Ford's much praised assembly-line efficiency and qualifies the myth of the American landscape in one thrust. Its low-key ironic grayness skewers landscape photography (as it was understood and praised in 1935) into the bargain: a gesture not of simple negation, but of critical purification, a refusal to accept shoddy goods passed off as culture, or jingoistic slogans paraded as truth.

And not just a refusal: when Evans's pictures are critical, as they frequently seem to be, they always offer, or at least imply, an admirable (if not modest) alternative. The brilliance of his own performance, the rigor and quality of his own examination of culture, the sharpness of his wit set the standard against which other achievements fall short. The assembly-line (in league with good old American salesmanship) may have made a mess of the Pennsylvania countryside, and landscape art may not have come up with much to describe, let alone understand, the true state of affairs, but this photograph knows its business well enough. As in the satirical prints of Hogarth and the mock epics of Pope, the accuracy and acuity of the diagnosis are often more reassuring than the conditions described: the world may be falling to pieces around the artist's head, but the line is sure and precise, and each couplet snaps smartly to a perfect close.

AFTER PHOTOGRAPHING in the Cape May parking lot for half an hour or so, Walker refreshed himself from the thermos of strong sweet tea he always had with him. Students were drifting up from time to time as he worked, but he did not allow their presence to distract him. One or two looked on as he examined his morning's haul, a small stack of glowing prints, the latest exposures still developing their full richness of color. He gave at least one to a student as a memento, but he declined to sign it with his full name.

We set out to catch the ferry to cross the Delaware, but the day's tone had been set. Every few hundred yards Walker would see something that drew his eye, and he would tell me to stop. We stopped for an ice cream cone sign, suspended high above the ground on a pole, a model stagecoach advertising a camp ground, a display of cast concrete figures at a roadside garden supply store (one of the cast elves looked like a benign Eisenhower), and for signs, including the oval serif *W* posted along railroad tracks to alert the engineer to blow the whistle for a crossing. We also stopped for examples of the regional warning to roving hunters, NO GUNING. I remember lots of gleeful chuckles as he bagged his finds.

I thought of our destination, the ferry, and its schedule. Walker kept calling for stops. By now we were separated from the other cars by miles, maybe by hours, but Walker's excitement seemed to increase with each new picture. I had not previously seen him so stimulated by making photographs. The closest to this behavior I had seen was watching him set out on some necessary errand, walking across a parking lot to make a telephone call, and stopping again and again, each time with great effort and excruciating slowness, to bend over and collect yet another detached pull-up for his already sizeable collection. That was relentless, almost grim, perhaps even an effort to postpone making the telephone call. This was exuberant, even manic. I recalled Agee's description near the beginning of *Let Us Now Praise Famous Men* of their discovery of a Negro church; Agee is certain Evans will break into it if he can't quickly find someone to give them permission to enter.

When we reached the ferry at last, Walker was feeling triumphant. He lent me the camera to make two pictures of him, against the sky, looking rather grand standing at the rail in his sunglasses and tweed jacket.

After that day I have only intermittent memories of Walker's photographic work on this trip. He went out with the students a few times, using Rolleiflexes, and in the evening, he ate and talked with them. Unfinished rolls of black-and-white film from these outings were still in two of the Rolleiflexes when they passed to me after his death a year and a half later.

On trips like this (as well as in his classes at Yale), his manner toward the students varied from student to student, and I suspect a survey of those who studied with him would yield a wide spectrum of opinions on his manners and his value as a teacher/example. He tolerated most students and was usually courteous – so courteous that in a few instances he might be said to have been 'paying court,' his term for the kind of attention a man gives to the object of a romantic interest. A few he was drawn to as potential artists, or at least competent photographers, and he treated them accordingly. Some he just couldn't abide and found reasons to ignore. One man who had displeased him found himself seated next to Walker at the long dining table in the motel

Evans: untitled
[NO GUNING sign
photographed near
Cape May, New Jersey,
October 17, 1973, in color]

restaurant in Accomac. For most of the meal Walker presented him with the narrow expanse of his tweed-covered back as he chatted amiably with students in the other direction.

Others found him more accessible than they had dared imagine, even charming. He tended to notice well-bred young men and the women, of course (the students on these trips were mostly graduate students in their early 20s or older), but the pattern of his interests was not, I noticed, easily predictable by conventional social preferences: one of the students who caught his interest on this trip was Asian, and another was an ex-Marine. Both were enthusiastic photographers of subjects more or less in Walker's line, and male.

The only other pictures I remember his making on this trip were in black-and-white, but not with a Rolleiflex. They were two 8 x 10 negatives made of me, at close range, on the front porch of Walker's motel cabin.

These pictures resulted from my request to photograph him. I had photographed him with a view (large negative) camera several times, but not since his beard had grown so full.

Also I think I had a new view of him after watching his performance on 17 October. So I asked him to sit on the porch, his face just out of the direct sun, and I set up my 8 x 10 view camera on its tripod in front of him. I tried one or two just as he was, hair touseled by the wind, from a medium distance: these record head and shoulder down to the third or fourth button of the shirt. Then he combed his hair and I moved closer, closer than I had ever tried to come to a subject with a large view camera.

I tried half a dozen exposures from this distance, sometimes moving the camera slightly between exposures, and other times making variations with the same framing. Even though we were in bright open shade with patches of unfiltered sunlight visible in part of the picture, the focus is shallow. The lens is extended a long way from the film in these closeups, which necessitates an increase in exposure, and I used a fast shutter speed to avoid movement – 1/25th of a second, I think, so the lens diaphragm is open quite wide; a lens of 14-inch focal length doesn't give a wide range of sharpness at this distance at any aperture.

Accomac, Virginia, 1973

Evans: untitled [Jerry Thompson, Accomac, Virginia], 1973

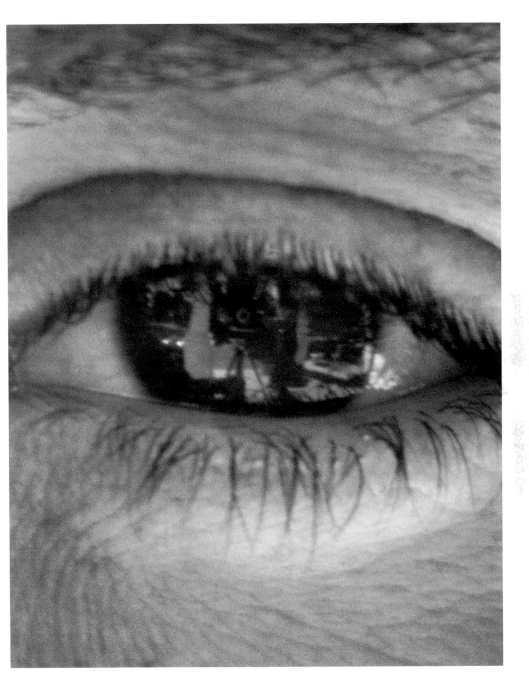

Detail of left eye, preceding picture

I was paying attention to small changes in his expression as well as to the details of framing, so I continued making exposures until I thought I might have a good one or two. Walker then said he would do one of me. I couldn't date his last picture done with an 8 x 10 camera, but it might have been as much as twenty years earlier. I had suppressed a laugh when he answered a Dartmouth student's question about his use of this large camera. Do you still use the 8 x 10 view camera? the student had asked in 1972. Less and less, Walker had answered.

I sat down, his jacket still on the chair back, and he looked through the camera. He must have adjusted the focus, since with even so shallow a depth of field my eyelashes are as sharp as that lens allowed, as is the tiny figure visible in my left pupil. Only the sunstruck white beard represents the face, but the image gives a clear record of the tense stance – legs spread apart, a slight crouch rather like a fighter's, and the right arm extended, holding the short cable release.

Weeks later, when I showed him some results from this session, he glanced at the prints briefly, grunted, and set them aside, saying only, "I did better than you." Generosity in competition was not one of the gentlemanly attributes he had chosen to cultivate.

His trip to England had been a success, and this working trip to Virginia had also come off well, in spite of its rocky start. The whole autumn of 1973 followed this same happy course. It was a halcyon time, the longest pleasant, productive period of Walker's life during the years I knew him.

That autumn was in part a social season. It began the night he returned from England, on 19 September. I met him in New York when he arrived on the S.S. *France*, and we drove directly to Old Lyme. He decided we should have a guest for a welcome-home dinner at his house, so he called Mary Knollenberg, a sculptor, friend of many years, and a recent widow who lived across the river from Walker. She had visited during his recuperation the previous winter, and they enjoyed a long-standing good-natured competition on a number of issues, including artistic work, performance at golf (Walker had let his club membership lapse and sometimes played with Mary as her guest), who knew whom, and money.

At dinner he told of his adventures. He had stayed in the London flat of Robert and Caroline Lowell (Caroline was an old friend) and he had been invited out a good deal. He had been so busy in London that he scarcely managed to get away for a planned stay with a friend in Holland. He told one long story of a dinner party somewhere in London, attended mostly by stylish young people. He was a little hard of hearing and had not made out all the introductions clearly. At dinner his hostess seated him next to a young Englishman in jeans with a full Afro-style hairdo, a man whose name Evans understood to be Earl something. After an evening of lively conversation he said elaborate good-byes, being careful to use his dinner companion's name Earl several times. A little while later the hostess explained to Walker that Earl was not the name but rather the title of the peer Walker had been sitting next to all through the dinner.

We all three laughed at the story's conclusion. Mary said pointedly that Walker had told his story so well, and with such winning self-deprecation, that she forgave him the boast that was his reason for telling it – that he had hobnobbed with the aristocracy (Mary had an ancient edition of *Burke's Peerage* in her library at home). All three laughed again, but sometime before the evening was over Walker managed to remind Mary that her biggest problem was that she had too much money.

Their good-natured sparring continued at a string of evening parties that spread out over the autumn. Three or four times Mary came to dinner, bringing along a tall, striking niece (nicknamed Ippy for her resemblance to 'The Girl from Ipanema' of the 1960s popular song), whose husband was both pleasant to Walker and smart enough not to compete with him for the (momentary) attention of his young wife. During one of those evenings Walker made a series of pictures of three heads, close together. Mary, her niece, and I are the cast of his little drama. Potent (if not killing) glances shoot from one character to another, vectors realigning from picture to picture, and sometimes aimed at the eye behind the camera, making Walker the fourth character in this imagined play, which he might have titled *Flirtation, or Les Liaisons pas très dangereuses*.

Two or three other neighbors sometimes came to these parties. I would prepare what passed for the food – usually some kind of broiled beef to be served with baked potatoes and a vegetable that could be boiled in its plastic pouch. We served red wine, often selected by Walker. He sniffed it but never, during this time, took even a sip. He consoled himself with huge gooey desserts.

We had one of these parties almost every week during October and November. One of them, the Saturday nearest 3 November, celebrated Walker's seventieth birthday and included guests from New York as well as New Haven. For these parties the women always dressed up, and Walker was the image of a dandy in opera pumps, brightly colored trousers and contrasting bright socks, one of his beautiful English shirts worn with a cable-stitch sweater and ascot. In deference to his ambitions for these evenings, I usually managed to look a little better than the unkempt derelict who appears in most of his pictures of me.

Walker was visited in Old Lyme by writers, artists, and other photographers, as well as his Old Lyme neighbors. John Clellan Holmes, Jack Jessup, Leslie Katz, Emmet Gowin, Jill Krementz, and William Christenberry were among those who visited when I was around, and Lee Friedlander came several times. I was struck to see Walker behave a little like a kid brother during Friedlander's visits, asking the younger artist to tell about what he was involved in and admiring his ability to get things done. Walker seemed to me grateful for Friedlander's attention and pleased to have someone he could look up to and rely on. Friedlander had, after all, arranged for Walker to write an introduction to a collection of his pictures, and later managed the publication of a portfolio of Walker's pictures: both commissions brought Walker significant income. Years before, Walker told me, Friedlander had advised him about lenses and helped him to buy and set up an enlarger.

Walker had a trick of getting others to take responsibility for certain things, usually things having to do with getting along. He even managed this with someone as junior as I was. Not long after I began to spend a good amount of time in Old Lyme, perhaps as early as the spring of 1972, he began jokingly to call me 'Daddy' from time to time. Maybe an afternoon seemed particularly shapeless, or he had to accomplish three errands in two different places: some aspect of scheduling or necessity needing organizing, and he would get me to do it. Once I showed I had a plan, he would say something like, Do we have time for dessert, Daddy? This joking seemed to me entirely good-natured; we both laughed, and I was never aware of a sharp edge to his joke. With Walker, however, as with a few other greatly civilized members of his generation I met in later life, I was sometimes uncertain of his tone. At those moments I found myself unable to tell the difference between irony and direct statement, if there was a difference.

As I spent more time with him I began to think that his relationships with other people – in particular people he could learn something from or somehow use – were at least as complex as his many-leveled connection to the things he photographed and collected. I had already read (in John Szarkowski's 1971 essay) about his collaboration, if that's what it was, with John Brooks Wheelwright and Lincoln Kirstein. Together they had photographed Victorian architecture; Wheelwright and Kirstein found the examples and provided entree, but (according to Kirstein's account) Walker wanted to be left alone when it came to the actual making of the photographs. I also knew something about his partnership with James Agee in Alabama, though I didn't know until he told me that he never stayed with the farm families he photographed. He said he couldn't eat their food and preferred a hotel.

Gradually, as I asked him about this or that picture, I heard of other people who had been along with him at the time he made the photograph. When I asked how he had had the nerve to photograph three disgruntled-looking rough types lounging in a Lower Manhattan doorway, he said a sailor buddy of Hart Crane's had been with him as bodyguard and had even shown him some good places to work. The overstuffed New Year's Day chair (the image on the exhibition poster of the Museum of Modern Art) turned out to have been in the house of a friend's cook, whom he followed home, and an odd numbered storefront in Colorado – subject of a frequently exhibited photograph from the '60s – had been shown to him by a friend he was visiting.

I began to ask about pictures deliberately, to find out for myself who else had been along. My original notion was that the greatest pictures must have resuled from concentrated quests, acts of genius working in splended solitude. Wrong again. It was difficult to find any picture he had made while alone, or without having used someone else's knowledge or connections for access to the subject. Even when he made the great epic views from the cemetery in Easton, Pennsylvania, including the one with the large foreground cross – one of Walker's best-known pictures and a thundering artistic epiphany if ever he had one – someone else had been with him. I never found out from him who it was, but he had a picture of himself photographing in that cemetery on that day, and only someone with him – another photographer – could have made it.

I gave up my curious-question game after asking about his view of the breakfast room at Belle Grove plantation. This was one of the first pictures I had printed for him, and its ecstatic whiteness and soaring columns (pilasters, actually) had made a big impression on me. It was also one of the first pictures by Walker Evans I understood to be great, resonantly allusive and more than the simple beauty of its visual arrangement. Walker had visited Belle Grove in the company of his first wife Jane, whom he was then (1935) courting in New Orleans. I don't remember his description of that day's trip in any detail, but it sounded to me more like a picnic in the country than an artistic quest. He may even have said that they sat outside on the grass during the long exposure needed to photograph the breakfast room inside, the walls of which had been painted pink.

Not only did the presence of others not distract Walker, but company was helpful, even necessary, to his artistic work. The willingness to rely on others, and his ability to feed on what others knew and were – these traits, it seemed to me, must have helped him absorb and synthesize at least some of the stupefying breadth and comprehensive authority that characterize his work. During his working life he fell into the company of a long, distinguished line of buddies: Crane, Ben Shahn, Kirstein, Hemingway (briefly, but significantly, at least for Walker), John Cheever, Muriel Draper, Jan Leyda, Tom Mabry, Agee, Helen Levitt to name only a few, and all before 1940. At least some of the range of his work must have come, somehow, from them, through him. Like studying for a test by sleeping with a book under the pillow, I thought, but Walker never studied for a test, I suspected (certainly never for a public talk on his own work, when I knew him). Like God in the catechism and Popeye in the comic strip, he simply was what he was.

Evans, untitled [Coca-Cola shed in Accomac County,
Virginia, between Locustville and Wachapreague],
April 1, 1972

School crossing sign collected by Evans and
photographed at home under his direction,
1972 or '73

Evans, untitled [street arrow], 1973–74
The Metropolitan Museum of Art, Purchase,
Samuel J. Wagstaff Jr. Bequest and Lila
Acheson Wallace Gift, 1994. (1994.245.1)

Evans, untitled [detail of street lettering], September 16, 1974
The Metropolitan Museum of Art, Purchase,
Samuel J. Wagstaff Jr. Bequest and Lila Acheson
Wallace Gift, 1994. (1994.245.23)

Evans, untitled [detail of liquor store sign], 1973–74
The Metropolitan Museum of Art, Purchase,
Samuel J. Wagstaff Jr. Bequest and Lila Acheson
Wallace Gift, 1994. (1994.245.26)

Evans, untitled [Janet Byrd, Oberlin College],
January 22, 1974. Private Collection

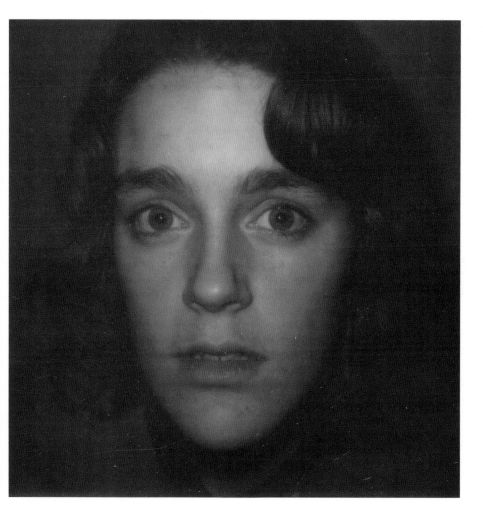

Evans, untitled [Jane Corrigan],
1973–74. Private Collection

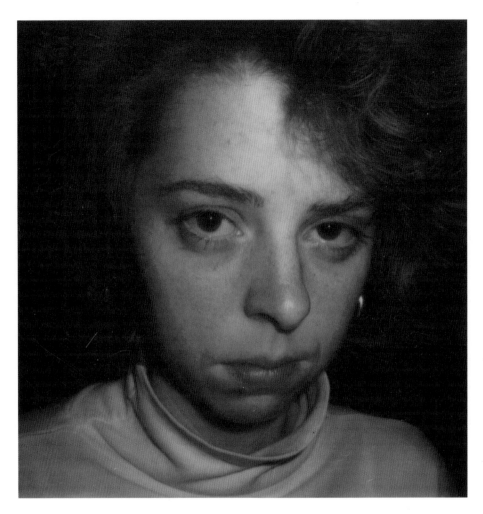

Evans, untitled [Nancy Shaver],
December 11, 1973. Private Collection

THROUGHOUT THE ACTIVE, social fall of 1973, Walker was regularly making pictures with his Polaroid SX-70. These small square color pictures he made so freely are related to his earlier work but often different in spirit. In photographing signs, for example, Walker had tended, both in his earlier work (as I have said) and in the early days of his work with the SX-70, to photograph the whole sign, sometimes at close range but nearly always including the entire sign and something of its context, either visual or intellectual. The resulting photographs have a literary or satirical component of meaning, often a rich one.

As viewers or readers of Evans, we have all been affected by the authoritative vision, the cumulative literary operation of the collection of pictures arranged with such powerful effect in the two sections of *American Photographs*. In that book, shapes present nameable *things*, things with histories and associations; the clash and cooperation among the meanings of these things provide much of the intellectual content of the book, which, as Lincoln Kirstein claims near the end of his afterword, amounts to a national epic, a genre not usually attempted in picture form.

But the book happened at a particular moment of Walker's working life, and even at that time he was making pictures that relied on other, less obviously literary qualities. Light and shadow patterns, geometrically active perspective, puzzling oddities he described on negative envelopes as surreal – these and other subjects that appear in his work from beginning to end consistently resist the literary interpretation that applies so nicely to the pictures in *American Photographs*. Indeed, it could be (and probably will be) argued that Walker Evans, during his forty-five years as a working photographer, tried out every major artistic style of the century, from late Romanticism and Cubism to Pop and Conceptual.

There is in his work – not just in many single pictures, but in the way he approached subjects, usually making many variants as he photographed them, and also in the way he subsequently printed and edited the results, frequently continuing not only to preserve but to print and exhibit multiple variants for years, sometimes using one version and sometimes another – a restless refusal to settle down and follow one thought to a finished conclusion. Running alongside the classical head-on lucidity, the cool precision generally taken to be his signature style, there is also a thread of deep anarchism, a stubborn unwillingness to accept a final resolution. He was, perhaps, so wary of shoddy goods that he was suspicious even when he himself was the supplier.

Nowhere does this anarchistic streak find freer play than in the Polaroids he made of signs during the last few months of his life. In October 1973 he photographed a NO GUNING [sic] sign in New Jersey, standing back far enough to include something of its woodland setting, and the picture is as funny and as oddly beautiful as any of the JESUS SAVES signs he photographed in black-and-white decades earlier. By the spring of 1974, however, he had begun daily outings to photograph things nearer at hand, and these subjects, these signs, are often treated differently.

One midday in Old Saybrook, a town near Old Lyme he frequently visited to run errands and eat lunch, he worked on a collection of arrows painted on the roadway of a complex intersection near the center of the town. He chose not to concentrate on photographing the entire arrangement or its setting, but to close in on it, dissecting it and photographing it in pieces. In his pictures, arrows point in different directions, sporting with each other and with the borders of the picture. Walker is not interested here in any single view or statement, much less in the historical or social significance of the site or style of decoration. He is interested in the play, in the action afforded by this graphic display: *the direct, instinctive, bemused sensuality of the eye in play.*

During the spring of 1974 he came regularly to New Haven, and in the fall we began to share an apartment on Park Street, near the Yale School of Art but also near the downtown part of the city. When in New Haven, Walker usually made daily outings centered around lunch, outings during which he would walk for a few blocks with his camera. By heading one way he could reach the School of Art and nearby off-campus restaurants within five minutes or so. A walk of a similar length in another direction would take him up Crown Street toward the (then) mostly run-down urban center of New Haven. This direction led to a number of closed-up vacant buildings, stores on their last legs, and parking lots on the sites of other buildings that had been demolished.

The entire area was rich in crude hand-lettered signs, graffiti, and other graphic residue of great interest to Walker. He explored this territory repeatedly and regularly, sometimes photographing whole signs but frequently entering the signs as he did the intersection at Old Saybrook, to dissect and reconstruct them. In these new pictures Walker went far beyond the role of *selecting*, which had occupied him during his recent period of collecting signs and making his odd home photographs of them. This new aggressive approach to his subject did not ignore or deny the simple beauty of these signs, but Walker was no longer content merely to copy and present this beauty. His intervention adds an extra layer of meaning to that already displayed by the sign itself and pushes his work with this subject-matter into new territory.

Pieces of words form new words not imagined by the signs' makers, and pieces of letters play with other whole and partial letters in an orgy of semantic exuberance, clearly related to the wordplay and joking that sprinkled Walker's conversation and letters. And almost always color, light, and framing are full partners in the romp. In these pictures, finally, his recent fascination with signs – the interest that for two or three years had been dispersed among field photographs, his puzzling home records of displaced objects, and his collecting of the things themselves – all this interest was concentrated and focussed.

We see in these pictures the direct, instinctive, bemused eye operating at full tilt, playing for all its worth. The pictures show the final, complete theft of the signs he lifted: a sure and successful use, the full mastery of a subject that had come to him gradually, through a series of different stages, none of which pointed clearly ahead to the next. Through all this long gestation period, some of it quite difficult, physically and mentally (not to mention financially) for Walker, he had held his concentration. He continued to pay attention and not merely to walk through old motions familiar from years of habit. What I saw for the first time in October 1973 had a glorious conclusion in the fall of 1974. Then, during evening editing sessions that sometimes followed chaotic, dispiriting days, I watched Walker look through, sometimes sign and date, and occasionally imprint with his inked thumb freshly made, beautiful, brightly colored treasures, strange and wonderful fruit of a late, unexpected harvest.

NEW HAVEN OFFERED not only stimulating graphic displays,
but also people to spend time with. Walker had a few close
friends in Old Lyme, but only a few, and they lived far apart.
In New Haven he had close friends of nearly a decade's standing
at the School of Art, and friends elsewhere in the university as
well; the continuous arrival of visiting faculty and fresh students
promised the appearance of more. We had talked about sharing
an apartment in New Haven since the previous fall, when I had
lived a few months as his guest. The following spring I had taken
an apartment with a friend nearer my own age, and Walker had
stayed there a few times as a sort of trial run. It had worked out,
so he and I rented the place on Park Street.

The fall of 1974 got off to a good start for Walker. He moved
into our two-bedroom apartment gradually, spending a few nights
a week there at first. We brought in some furniture from Old
Lyme – a kerosene lamp or two, two cane-bottomed and one
ladderback chair, an upholstered chair, and what he called a
Madame Récamier couch. A pine trestle table I had made in 1971
for my student apartment was our dining table. Walker slept on
the couch in his bedroom, until I got a folding rollaway for him.
I used a mattress on the floor on my smaller bedroom. I
contributed a Morris chair (sub-Stickley) from the Waterbury
Goodwill Store and a stack of architect's file drawers from a local
junk shop. We used my college radio/stereo and a set of stainless
steel flatware (place settings for twelve) given me by a favorite
aunt when I started as a student at Yale. We split the rent.

The apartment house was a newish but solid highrise with a
doorman and plaster walls, fancy by my standards, and it amused

Evans's bedroom,
111 Park Street,
October, 1974

Walker. He got into the spirit of our ad hoc decor (he called it
Upper Bohemia), placing a few choice dump-pickings around
the mostly empty living-dining area and mounting a child's
bicycle, partly crushed in what may have been a gruesome
accident, on the wall over the table. He also bought two framed
offset reproductions for the bare walls, a Gottlieb and another
I can't recall, perhaps a Klee. One afternoon during the early

days of that apartment I came in and found the radio blaring (he had marked his favorite classical station on the dial with permanent black marker for easy tuning) and Walker attempting to open or close the sliding doors to the balcony. Part of them lay at his feet. Come in, he said heartily, I'm just engaging in a little home dis-repair.

I had been regularly seeing a young woman named Jane Corrigan since the previous winter, and her frequent presence in the apartment also added to our little household. Walker enjoyed her company, and we often went out as a threesome. We had a few evening parties, but nothing so regular as the 'fall season' of the previous year. For one thing, Walker's New Haven friends were a larger, more varied group than the Old Lyme circle. For another, his involvement in the life of the Park Street apartment was less continuous than life in the country household had been the previous fall. There was something going on in Old Lyme, a deal of some sort that often required his attention and presence.

As the end of the previous summer had approached, Walker had stayed in Old Lyme rather than travel to England as he had done the two preceding years. I had been photographing and staying in New York, and I knew his studio and files were being put in order by a visitor, Bobbi Carrey, a young woman who was experienced at organizing archives. She had been recommended by Davis Pratt, Curator of Photographs at the Fogg Art Museum of Harvard University. When I saw Walker toward the end of the summer, however, he referred mysteriously to a big sale, and to an Englishman in a Rolls-Royce who was going to give him a lot of money.

He didn't tell me any details of this proposed transaction, but at certain times he had to be in Old Lyme, and he went alone.

I had work of my own – by this time I was trying to find someone else who could take over the work of printing Walker's negatives – and I never thought of myself as his constant companion. Consequently I didn't press him for information, though I did wonder what was going on. Even I, with little business experience, realized his judgments were considerably less certain in financial than in artistic matters.

In October, shortly after a Yale traveling workshop Walker led (again with my assistance) to Martha's Vineyard, I noticed he suddenly had several $10,000 cashier's checks. With characteristic financial savvy he stored most of them uncashed in a vault of a

Upper Bohemia, 111 Park Street, October, 1974

bank across the street from the apartment. Every few days he would go across the street and fill up his money belt with a few fifties and hundreds. The studio in Old Lyme, which had been clean and filled with neat stacks of museum storage boxes when I had last seen it, was now mostly empty.

In spite of this enigmatic distraction, Walker settled into life in New Haven pretty comfortably, spending more and more time there as the fall progressed. He even found time to attend a faculty meeting at the School of Art, where he sat happily enough circling the names of his friends on his xeroxed copy of the agenda and scribbling cartoon-like portraits in the margins (along with the message, "my new pen writes well"). Probably he and I joined a faculty group for dinner after the late-afternoon meeting. Restaurant meals, invitations to have dinner at the homes of friends, an occasional date, and a few evening parties on Park Street helped fill the time when he was not walking the streets with his camera, traveling to speak at colleges, or going out to Old Lyme.

Social events were also occasions for him to photograph. Almost as soon as he started using his SX-70 he began to make close portraits. He had brought a number back from his trip to England, and he made pictures of students when he traveled to lecture. The camera is well adapted to portraits. It focusses close, and the flash sits just above the lens – there is no separate viewfinder that a flash so close to the lens might block – so shadows resulting from the flash are small and narrow, serving merely to emphasize the lower contours of facial forms. Also, the color balance of the film yields pleasing skin colors (probably not by accident); they tend to be a little warm, making the faces appear healthy, full of blood and life. The illumination of the flash falls off quickly, typically yielding close-ups that show a strongly volumetric face whose margins begin to fade into the surrounding warm darkness.

Picture-taking at parties did not, however, always produce great art. Walker took me and our friend Jane to an evening party in the fall of 1974, probably early November, at the apartment of a poker partner of an Art School friend. He was a scientist, his girl friend a nurse, and most of the guests were graduate students or teaching assistants with a common interest in Eastern European folk dancing.

Later in the evening, after dinner, most of the guests began to dance. Walker had brought his camera, which when folded fitted smoothly into the side pocket of the tweed jackets he usually wore. I watched him press the exposure button repeatedly, as if the act of pressing the button might magically make the life around him turn into a coherent picture.

But it was late at night, hours since his most recent rest period, and he had drunk several glasses of wine. (He had not, during the time I knew him, taken even a tiny amount of alcohol, not even hard sauce on deserts, until late summer 1974, when he began to drink wine.) The pictures from this session show flashes of whirling color, a face here, a fragment of a gesture there. They give only rough hints of what Walker may have been looking at.

Not since the very beginning of his working life had the progress of Walker's photographic work followed so closely the contours of his daily life, and never had he worked with less artistic and emotional distance from his subject. In earlier years he had often used a complex apparatus, such as an 8 x 10 view camera with a triple-convertible lens, or the boxy Speed Graphic with its two shutters, inaccurate viewfinder, and separate tiny sight for rangefinder focussing. Both cameras required considerable attention from the photographer.[3] He had gone on expeditions, or 'working trips,' as he called them, to find his subjects, and he frequently made use of work rituals, such as riding the subway with a concealed camera, or setting up a Rolleiflex on a tripod fixed in a downtown location in a Midwestern city. He had even used a right-angle finder and a false poser to photograph his real subjects on the sly.

In 1974, however, he was taking his camera and photographing almost everywhere he went – once he even tried to take it along on a brief hospital stay (for nosebleed), but a nurse warned him against having portable valuables in his room. Looking through the bright, large viewfinder was hardly different from simply looking, and the automatic camera required no adjustment except focussing. He was working at close range with subjects he was somehow connected to: people he knew and liked, girls he had crushes on, old friends. He was always interested in what was going on when he pressed the shutter release, but the pictures that resulted do not always have the power and coherence of his best work.

Sometimes, though, they do. Some of the SX-70 portraits have an intimacy, or a reaching for intimacy, that recalls a few earlier portraits, pictures that stand in contrast to many of Walker's other, more distant portraits (which have their own, different power).

In a few early pictures – one of Lincoln Kirstein, which views him from slightly above, his face and eyes turned up toward the camera, and a little-known 8 x 10 vertical half-figure of a hitchhiker by the side of a Mississippi road who also appears, in a better-known picture, photographed from a distance, thumbing a ride with a companion and suitcase – there is visible an attitude of beseeching, a yearning for something the pictures do not spell out. In the case of the hitchhiker I suspect this yearning might

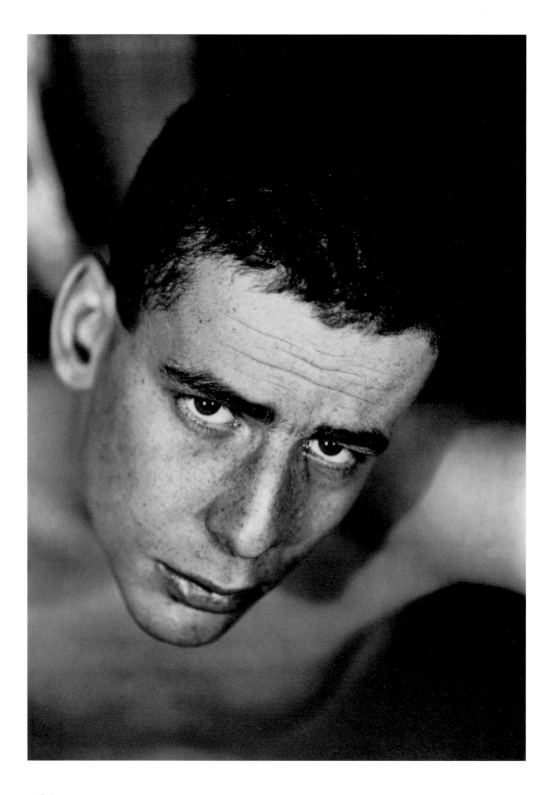

Evans: untitled [Mississippi hitchhiker], 1935–36

Evans: untitled [Lincoln Kirstein], ca. 1931

be for the good opinion of the well-dressed stranger and his fancy camera, and for the immortality their presence promises to confer.

In other of Walker's pictures of people – I think of the picture of the landlord that opens *Let Us Now Praise Famous Men* – the human subject appears as an object to be examined, held at a cool distance in an emotional as well as a spatial sense. In these other two examples, though, the examined human subjects show a desire to bridge that distance: each offers a response that has been accepted (even if not encouraged) by the man behind the camera.

A related quality of openness, even interest, appears in a number of Walker's Polaroid portraits from 1973 and 1974, and this appearance suggests to me a strong yearning for human contact across the camera, not just artistic contact. The subjects often look as if they are about to speak or laugh, or had paused for a moment during animated conversation or serious reflection. They seem open and connected to the camera in a way that calls attention to the man behind it.

Some of the pictures he made of the earnest, awkward students he met at lectures are almost satirical, but in many of the portraits of this time, it seems to me, his aim is not to make a comment or a point about his subjects, but to produce a kind of surrogate creation, a work of art that might somehow substitute for the close, living presence of the original.

When Walker and I talked, especially late at night, he had a trick of speaking about people who interested him. He would contrive to say the person's name again and again, luxuriously drawing out the syllables (especially of women's names) as if the act of saying the names, of having them in his mouth, gave him pleasure. He would use his agile intellect to elaborate complex motives for simple things done by the subjects of his attention, and he would speculate about possible (but not likely) adventures with these hypothetical companions. Sometimes he would simply list all the girls he was currently interested in, saying their names slowly, one at a time. All of this involved repeating the names endlessly; at the time I sensed a wizardry in action. In some ancient pre-rational way he was drawing on these people, gaining strength from them, using the fact of their existence to bolster his own.

I think some of his late portraits served him in the same way as those late-night mental exercises. They were expressions of deep need, but also exertions of power, both as an artist and as a man; they were highly charged but essentially benign, a relatively harmless means of possession.

He made a dozen or more pictures of some subjects, often making a number of variants that are nearly – but not quite – identical. The responses he chose to record are often extraordinarily complex, and expressed in nuances of considerable delicacy. Some of the subjects of these portraits, I think, must have begun to sense the power and seriousness of this close scrutiny, this attempted possession. In these faces the attentive viewer can discern the beginnings of hesitation, a small qualification of the easy openness so remarkable in these portraits as a group, a hint of pulling back that adds a note of reservation, suspicion, even fear. That note underscores the difficulty, even hopelessness, of his situation at this late period, and makes it impossible for me to look at these pictures, even at poor photocopies of them, without being touched to the heart. Looking closely at a dozen or twenty of these late portraits is a powerfully affecting experience, especially for a viewer who values the psychological qualities of a portrait as much as the visual design of the picture.

Walker made as many as six hundred close portraits between late 1973 and the end of November 1974. To my eye at least, a number could hang with confidence alongside the great portrait he made of Allie Mae Burroughs in 1936.[4]

The importance to him of this work would be hard to overstate. These pictures summoned up and concentrated his dwindling energies; their vital importance to him – vital is not an exaggeration – accounts for the power of the strongest of them. As in the spare, pared-down late landscapes of Atget, and in the cloud studies of Stieglitz, the viewer is witness to a kind of genius (blended, in Walker's case, with a titanic sensuality) confronting the inevitability of death. In 1974 Walker, though only seventy, was an old man, and he knew it.

Evans making a close portrait (of Mercedes Matter) at a party in Bethany, CT, October, 1973

ALL THROUGH THAT autumn he continued to photograph with his SX-70s (he eventually had three). He spent much of his time in New Haven, and continued to work on signs and found objects as well as human subjects. He had an idea for an alphabet book: it was to be 9 x 12 inches in size and present a good picture of each letter. To help this project along we taped his letter pictures up on the walls of his bedroom in a line. A picture I made, probably in October, of that wall shows gaps and some duplications. There are lots of E's and W's.

There was a new development in his portrait pictures, too. In addition to the portraits he was making at parties and lectures, he began to arrange sittings – scheduled sessions when the subject would come to the apartment. Walker would make a number of pictures, sometimes involving alteration if not a change of costume.

I never watched any of these sessions, but he told me he was excited about a new twist in his work. He described the sittings as acting, and said he would instruct or direct his subjects as he made the pictures. There were perhaps a dozen of these sittings, sometimes more than one with the same person, and I believe all the subjects were young women.

By mid-November, Walker was clearly having a hard time. He complained of various physical problems, which might be symptoms of some new serious ailment, and he was more restless than usual. His manner had acquired a new urgency that sometimes resembled desperation, as if he were looking for something he increasingly despaired of finding. He was obviously drinking more: his occasional glass of wine had increased to a number that would have a strong effect on a man with so little body weight – I doubt that he weighed as much as 120 pounds at this time – and he had begun to drink when alone.

Eventually his friends, I, and even Walker himself decided he needed some kind of help. He wanted a private hospital that used drugs rather than talk therapy as a means of drying out, but neither I nor anyone else could find one. Many of the small private hospitals that used to treat alcoholics had gone out of business, and the remaining ones I could find out about all used some kind of counseling based on AA.

Time passed, and began to drag. On several evenings I sat with Walker and a loyal friend or two through a difficult meal, prepared by me, as we watched him consume as much as possible of the allotted bottle of wine, a recording of Erik Satie or Fats Waller helping to fill the frequent silences. On one evening when I sat with him to edit recent pictures, he asked for a glass of beer because there was nothing else in the apartment to drink.

Finally his fill-in psychiatrist (the first had taken a leave from his practice to write a book on creativity) saw Walker when he was particularly low and recommended an evaluation at the psychiatric unit of Yale-New Haven Hospital. They could do a full mental and physical examination, he said, and find out what was troubling him. There might be some physical cause. Both desperate, we agreed to make an appointment and waited for the time to arrive.

The night before (or perhaps a night or two earlier), trying to find something diverting to do, we decided to take a beachcombing find to my downtown studio so that Walker could try some pictures of it there. I had a loop of gray background paper set up, and we put the object, a float from a lobster pot, on the paper. Walker held up the camera and made one exposure, using the flash. Then, characteristically, he readjusted the LIGHTER/DARKER dial, the camera's only adjustment except for focus, and tried again. Then he reset the dial in the other direction, made a third bracket, and he was finished. In an attempt to break the silence of the gloomy ride back to the apartment, I said, At least you did a little work. Work, he snapped, that wasn't work – refusing once again to accept shoddy goods. And he lapsed into the silence that increasingly characterized his time with me. Sometime that night he may have quoted a sentence from Huxley, as he did from time to time at this stage: *I crave oblivion.*

I took him in to Yale-New Haven when the scheduled hour arrived. He was unhappy but resigned to this necessary step. I left as he was beginning the mandatory idiotic admissions interview.

When I returned a few hours later I found him in a high rage. He had gone up to the door, tried it, and discovered he was in a locked ward. He demanded to go home at once. Home to what? I asked, recalling the debilitating chaos of the previous days. We began to argue loudly, he wanting out, I denying him permission to leave, a parodic inversion of our first interview three years earlier. Our voices were so loud that the people in charge telephoned, and managed to reach the psychiatrist, who came. After a brief look at us both he announced his intention to commit one of us; as far as he could tell, he said, it was an even choice.

He then spoke briefly with Walker alone in a small office and Walker agreed to commit himself voluntarily for observation and evaluation. We said a formal good-bye, I left, and never afterward enjoyed his trust or confidence. There were other ties, though, and I was still responsible for a good portion of his daily affairs. Where I lived was still more or less his home. I kept in close touch. We both knew that when he left the hospital it would most likely be to live with me, at least for a while.

A day or two later he fell and broke his right collarbone. He could no longer hold a camera (or sign his name), and he had to be transferred to a medical ward. There he contracted pneumonia. He was regularly visited by many friends and colleagues, and of course by me; gradually alcohol and psychiatry took a back seat to a broken bone and infection. When his condition was 'stabilized,' he was recommended for discharge to a rehabilitation hospital.

Several friends worked with me to choose Gaylord Rehabilitation Hospital in nearby Wallingford, and we pitched the choice to Walker by telling him that Eugene O'Neill had been there. I went with him to enroll, and to see him given a furious dressing-down by a Filipino staff doctor. The hospital's goal was to get patients back on their feet and into life, not to coddle them, and the doctor upbraided Walker sharply for contributing to his own present condition. With a glance at me he said, If I were his son I would break his leg before I would let him walk across the street to the bar. Walker lay glumly on the bed of his new room.

Mary Knollenberg, his old friend and verbal sparring partner, was with us. As the doctor left she offered, "Well, Walker, I guess he told *you*!," thrusting gently in deference to her weakened friend. Walker's parry was feeble. The best he could do was to mutter, The Filipinos are a mongrel race. Two of us laughed.

He improved, and I continued to visit as one might an aged parent – not to accomplish any bit of business, but just to be there. He was responsive, but there was a hard canniness in his conversation with me that was new. He was trying to make the best of his situation, and he was careful not to give anything away that might work to his disadvantage.

Once I walked in to find the dealers who had bought all his prints – the Rolls-Royce had been prominent in the parking lot. One was George Rinhart, a scholar and dealer who was not English but drove a Rolls. The other was Thomas Bergen, who lived in England but was in fact an American. In his enthusiasm at the prospect of this deal Walker had apparently conflated all these facts into the "Englishman in a Rolls Royce" he had told me about earlier. This sale would bring him, within a year, $100,000, a round sum I decided he must have fixed on at some point (probably about 1930) as all the money he could ever need. Perhaps he felt that this deal was so good that his mind raced ahead to make it perfect: the money would come not from an ordinary businessman or investor, but from a rich Englishman. Miss Havisham, not Magwitch, would be his financial savior.

The two men had brought some papers for Walker to sign, including an agreement substituting a rubber stamp for the signature his injured arm prevented him from applying as liberally as they had hoped he might. Walker agreed with them that they had come up with a handsome stamp design.

After a couple of weeks at Gaylord he was strong enough to try a weekend visit to the home of his friends Norman and Connie Ives, a home with more stability and order than were available in Upper Bohemia. After this experimental overnight I arrived to take him back to Gaylord. I found him sitting on a sofa wearing, with sheepish amusement, a pair of striped Capri pants. He had wet his own trousers, and, since Norman's were too big, he had put on a pair of Connie's. He was in good spirits: there had been no disaster greater than the wet pants, and he would be released soon.

Back at Gaylord I followed as he walked with impressive determination through the long corridors, forcing himself to take big strides. I recalled his walks on the beach in 1973 and saw a glimmer of hope. He asked me to get in touch with Ginni Hubbard. She had had a child about a year earlier and had recently moved from Florida, where Walker had most recently visited her. We located her, and Walker asked her to come and live with him in New Haven. She arrived about the time Walker was discharged, 7 February, 1973. We had a welcome-home party on Park Street, attended by several friends. Our odd ad-hoc household now included Ginni, her 15-month-old son, and a nurse's aide, around the clock at first and later during the day only.

Ginni and Ezra moved into what had been my room. I kept my things there and stopped by a couple of times most days, but I slept at a friend's place. Visitors came by, often at night. One evening a group of friends, including a publisher and an expert printer, both old friends of Walker's, brought a dinner – steaks and baked potatoes – from Kaysey's, a local swell's steakhouse and (since his windfall) one of Walker's favorite restaurants.

He had by now talked to me about some of the details of his big sale. He had sold all the prints in his studio (including photographs by other artists), along with an option to purchase his negatives. He seemed to think the option was his to exercise or not, but it was a purchaser's, not a seller's, option. For the time being, he had agreed not to make any more prints from his negatives.

His publishing friends were working on a revival and improvement of the gravure printing process, which produced prints they felt could be as fine as or even finer than the silver prints Walker had made and sold for years. As we discussed this it became obvious that there was a particular advantage: the gravure printer starts with a print rather than with a negative.

Thus Walker could produce new prints of his pictures without breaking his agreement.

I remember much merriment and high spirits around the rickety table. Walker sat at the head, chain-smoking and occasionally saying, Really! or Yes – without, it seemed to me, any real connection to the conversation, even though he was fond of the visitors and glad they were there.

Nothing came of this plan during Walker's lifetime. He began to focus what energies he had on a speaking date he had made earlier with Radcliffe College. It was for early April, and he intended to try to keep it.

Apart from an occasional reference to this date, the days were interchangeable – a blur of nurse's aides, visits from friends and well-wishers, and the rare evening out, all sprinkled with brief periods of lucid conversation. Mostly Walker seemed to drift into or out of what was going on, according to his interest. He spent a lot of time in his room, and he smoked almost constantly. One of the aides had a boyfriend who could get marijuana, which Walker enjoyed. Oblivion.

We made a trip to Old Lyme to see about his negatives; there was a domestic squabble that required my spending a night in a chair in his room (for his protection, he said); an agent of the dealer who then owned the prints from the last sale (the deal changed hands once or twice during Walker's lifetime) visited, leaving behind a contract offering Walker a lifetime monthly stipend in lieu of the (large) balance of the sum they had agreed. I attempted (with partial success) to get Walker's help in editing my own pictures for a show I was having. There were other small dramas. But the main concern was the trip to Radcliffe in Cambridge, which was to be Walker's trial reentry into the outer world.

On 8 April, I picked up his train ticket and went to the apartment to take him to the station. Other friends had made arrangements for him to be met and taken around in Boston. When I arrived about noon, he was neither dressed nor packed. I put some things into a shoulder bag while the aide helped him dress. After a final snack, my eye again on the clock, we headed down to get into my van.

We drove the few minutes to the station, and I left the car at the front door, illegally, to walk with Walker, as fast as we could, toward the platform. (Ramps and wheelchairs were not so readily available in 1975 as they are in 1997.) At last I ran ahead, up some stairs, to try to hold the train. I reached the platform just in time to see the train, its doors closed, jerk and begin to move. Walker was behind me, halfway up the stairs to the platform. He dropped his head and shambled toward the nearest seat. After I checked on his ticket he said he wanted to go to a nearby steakhouse to eat, but then decided to have a sandwich at the station to save energy. He curled up on the plastic seat and began to doze as we waited for the next train to Boston.

A few telephone calls led to alteration of the arrangements for picking him up in Boston, and the friend in charge of that also found a Yale student willing to ride up on the train with Walker. This young man, an undergraduate I knew, showed up at the station, got a ticket, and took charge of Walker, whom I left drinking tea on the platform.

The next night Walker returned by train alone. I met him at the platform. A porter, lavishly tipped for the kindness, handed him down from the train, and he walked unsteadily with me to the car. He could not step up into the high van without help, so I lifted him in, minding his right arm. There had been no student portraits on this trip, satirical or otherwise.

Boston had been a great success; he was surprised at how easy that was. Just opened his mouth and said whatever came into his head. They were smart kids, had gotten a good talk out of him. He had learned how to do it, to take it easy, not to push himself too much.

As we entered the apartment he held up his arms in mock triumph, a familiar (but not recently seen) comic gesture suggesting also blessing, salutation, surprise. He went into his room and retired for a rest. I left, to return later, about 9 p.m.

Walker had thrown up. We had a brief, grimly funny discussion about whether that was possible, given the amount of abdominal surgery he had undergone, and then talked about the day's events, or at least those he chose to tell me about. Since his return home he had had a call from an English friend, Valerie Lloyd, a curator at the National Portrait Gallery in London about my age, who had most recently visited at Christmas when Walker had been in Yale-New Haven Hospital. They had a good talk, he said, and she was going to fly over in the summer and take him back with her. He had learned how to travel; getting away had been a good idea. They would advertise for a live-in couple to help them. There would be work for him in England. He might do a book on the English face.

He was sitting up in bed, smoking and holding a cup of tea, talking about things that would give him pleasure. He was alert, his mind active. I thought he might just be turning yet another corner, one more time. I left more encouraged about his prospects than I had been for a long time.

Two or three hours later I got a call telling me he had suddenly lost consciousness and been taken to the hospital emergency room by Ginni and a neighbor, a young intern or resident. I went immediately, and three or four others came as well. One doctor who had treated Walker was already there; he recognized me from office visits and came over. Walker had had a stroke – a cerebral event, said the doctor with unintended irony, making a tragic pun for an audience now diminished by one. Walker would not regain consciousness. All I could think to say in response to this was, Better than some, I guess. Better than *most*, returned the doctor with conviction, looking me in the eye briefly but directly before glancing down to step over a mop pail as he left. He had done what he could, which was mainly to reassure all present that no single event of the last few hours or days could have caused the stroke.

By early morning, the Connoisseur of Chaos, author of one of the great bodies of photographic art of the century we shared, and my close, difficult friend, was dead. May he rest in peace, now that his work – not just a collector's horde of expensive prints, but all the tens of thousands of negatives he left behind – has entered the collection of one of the world's great museums. May the pictures be looked at forever, and may they be studied and written about endlessly, or at least until we have some proper idea of the significance and range of his achievement. But may he rest in peace – that is to say, unvexed by meddlesome studies that dwell on messy personal details and ignore the complex greatness of his work, and its central role in any reasonable account of his life. And cursed be any whose inept, reductive, or mean-spirited scribblings disturb that well-earned rest.

111 Park Street,
late April, 1975

Notes to the text

1 "The Reappearance of Photography", Hound and Horn, October–December 1931. This brief essay describes how the power and vitality of early photography were submerged as self-conscious artist-photographers embraced the medium around the turn of the century. Evans does not apply the quoted words to any particular image, but contrasts them to his characterization of turn-of-the-century art photography: "a quaint evocation of the past." He clearly intends the words quoted in my text to apply to his ambitions in photography, which by 1931 he was already beginning to realize.

2 These are my words written more than twenty years after my last contact with Evans. Scholars and other close readers may want to have spelled out, here and now, more of what led me to these conclusions than can readily be fitted into the flow of a brief narrative.

In taking my long, close look at Evans's pictures and other work, my observations have been shaped by the experience of Walker I am trying to describe in this text, and this experience supplied many telling glosses. His conversation was riddled with jokes and asides – comments on the behavior of friends, on the preposterous fraudulence of some news report or radio advertising jingle we both heard, on the value of this or that cultural shibboleth – suggesting skepticism, to put it mildly, about the quality of our dominant culture. He referred to himself so many times as an 'anarchist' that I ceased to take it as completely a joke. I never thought he wanted to join up with those desperate types who threw actual bombs, but I did think he shared something of their outrage and disgust at the kind of world industrial capitalism had brought into being. It was not for nothing that he so often cited Baudelaire as a major influence;

I had once seen, among his early (1926) translations from the French, his rendering of a section of *Paris Spleen*, Baudelaire's collection of acid prose sketches of modern life.

He wrote things down from time to time – notes to himself, a few of which I saw and registered at the time. One page I saw was undated but written in a free, later script rather than the tight hand I remember from the early negative envelopes. It contained observations such as "Education no good, especially higher education" and "This period is a decadent one, and a young man who appears destructive [something I couldn't read] gone to hell now is often likely to be healthier than you are".

And – to step just this once away from first-hand knowledge – as late as 1985 I learned of another conversational partner who noted a similar skeptical streak in Walker. That year Lincoln Kirstein gave me typescripts of some entries from his journals that concerned Walker. On 26 March 1931 he noted "One of W.E.'s convictions": "nothing good ever happens except by mistake".

What I have written distils my impression of this contrarian aspect of Walker's thought – not all his thought, just one aspect of it. My attempt to describe this current is as accurate, I believe, as anything I was able to observe of him.

3 A fuller discussion of some of Evans's technical procedures and why they were of importance to him can be found in the introductory essay I wrote for *Walker Evans at Work* (New York/London, 1994).

4 I gave a lengthy account of this portrait in a talk at the Hyde Collection, Glen Falls, New York., in September 1994 (unpublished but circulated privately).

Selective Chronology

September 1971 – April 1975

1971	September	W E begin his last year as a regular faculty member of Yale University. Weekly classes on Mondays, School of Art; Tuesday College Seminar at Trumbull College
	October–November	Prepares exhibition at Yale Art Gallery – originally to be called "Walker Evans: An Anthology of Taste," it becomes instead "Walker Evans: Forty Years"
	9 December	Exhibition opens (runs through 19 January 1972)
1972	February	*Harvard Advocate* publishes a James Agee memorial issue with cover photograph and portfolio by W E
	February–March	Collects signs, photographs some at home
	March–April	Travels with two graduate students to Eastern Shore of Virginia. Photographs gingerbread twins in black-and-white, Coca-Cola shack in color and black-and-white
	27 May	Drives to Boston to deliver a set of prints sold to a Harvard student. His cameras stolen from his car but quickly recovered from a pawn shop
	August	Involved in details of having color prints made of home photographs of signs. Also photographs in black-and-white in New Hampshire for an upcoming show at Dartmouth College
	27 September	Arrives in New York aboard S.S. *France* from a brief trip to England
	early October	First traveling workshop with Yale advanced students in photography. Block Island was W E's initial choice, but Columbus Day weekend traffic precludes ferry reservations. Group travels to Martha's Vineyard, where W E explores Edgartown dump with students
	October–November	Artist in Residence, Dartmouth College. Meets with students and gives exhibition at Jaffe-Friede Gallery in the Hopkins Center. Collects signs and has them framed in Hopkins Center woodshop

1972	late November	Writes Thompson from Hitchcock Hospital, where he has been admitted for surgery. Virginia (Ginni) Hubbard has come to visit. W E wants some audio tapes he has made brought to him from Old Lyme
1973	3 January	Writes to Thompson from hospital expressing interest in acquiring a mat cutting machine to use in mounting new prints in overmats rather than by dry-mounting process
	mid-January	W E moves to Old Lyme to recover at home
	January–March	Continues experiments with audio tapes, resumes daily collecting trips to beach at Old Black Point, talks of a possible show of his collages (he favors Cordier-Ekstrom Gallery in New York)
	March	Visits Christopher and Evie Clarkson in Marigot, St. Martins, French Antilles
	21 April	Exhibition opens at Robert Schoelkopf Gallery, New York: black-and-white photographs 1929–1972
	up to 25 July	Visits in Decatur, Georgia, where he has his teeth fixed. Returns to Old Lyme via Bradley Airport in Hartford
	19 September	Returns from a trip to London via S.S. *France*. Welcome-home dinner with Thompson and Mary Knollenberg. Returns with a number of pictures made with a new color Polaroid camera, the SX-70, as well as rolls of 35mm and 120 black-and-white
	17 October	First working day of Yale traveling workshop. Photographs in Cape May, N.J., and en route to ferry across the Delaware
	3 November	W E's 70th birthday party in Old Lyme
	late December	Travels to Boston where he is met by Calvert Coggeshall, an old friend who takes him to Maine for Christmas holidays
1974	21 January	Writes from Oberlin College, where he is lecturing.
	c. 18–30 March	Visits University of Texas in Austin
	30 March–*c.* 15 April	Visits the Clarksons in St. Martins
	22 May	Receives Award for Distinguished Service to the Arts from the American Academy-Institute. Citation delivered by Lionel Trilling becomes introduction to Double Elephant portfolio of W E's pictures

	Summer	Bobbi Carrey visits in Old Lyme to put W E prints and negatives in order
	late Summer	Thompson meets W E at Robert Schoelkopf's summer house for dinner. W E has a glass of wine, permitted, he says, by his new psychiatrist
	September	W E and Thompson sign a lease of 8R, 111 Park St., New Haven, agreeing to split the monthly rent
	October	Travels with Yale students for a workshop on Martha's Vineyard. At almost exactly the same time, W E sells all black-and-white prints plus an option to buy his negatives
	October–November	Photographs in New Haven with SX-70, concentrating on signs and faces of friends and strangers
	November	Interviewed by James Mellow for *The New York Times*. The published article describes W E drinking (Thompson's) cognac. W E tells Thompson the cognac is gone because "that reporter from *The Times*" drank it all up.
	December	Checks into Yale-New Haven Hospital for examination and evaluation. Falls, breaking collarbone, and contracts pneumonia. Valerie Lloyd comes from England for a Christmas visit
1975	January	Discharged to Gaylord Hospital, a rehabilitation center in Wallingford
	7 February	Returns to 111 Park St. Ginni Hubbard and 15-months-old Ezra move in; nurses visit to attend W E
	March	Slow recovery. Current owner of W E's print collection visits to offer a monthly stipend for life in lieu of balance owed. W E declines.
	8 April	With difficulty takes a train to Boston to deliver a talk at Radcliffe that evening
	9 April	Returns to New Haven by train, shaky but triumphant. Suffers a late-night stroke and dies early next morning.

Index